Praise for

Why Do Vegetarians Eat Like That?

"This book answers every question [vegetarians] could ask about nutrition, diet and vegetarianism in an accurate, user-friendly format."
— **Sue Frederick, Editor,** *Delicious!* **Magazine**

"Packed with facts...concise, easy to read, and every page dispels another myth...."
— **Dick Allgire, News Anchor, KITV, News 4, Honolulu**

"I wish I had this book 20 years ago when I first went vegetarian."
— **Kim W. Stallwood, Editor-in-Chief,**
The Animals' Agenda

"Excellent...should be required reading for every dietitian and health professional..."
— **George Eisman, M.Sc., R.D., Member, American Dietetic**
Association; Director, The Association of
Vegetarian Dietitians and Nutrition Educators

"Answers all the questions people ask when considering or explaining vegetarianism."
— **Ingrid E. Newkirk, Chairperson,**
People For The Ethical Treatment Of Animals

"A great introduction for those considering the transition to vegetarianism."
— **Ron Pickarski, C.E.C., Chef;**
Author of *Friendly Foods*

"Great responses to...hundreds of questions that vegetarians frequently encounter."
— **Jennie O. Collura, President,**
North American Vegetarian Society

"David Gabbe has drawn together a guide...to show you how easy [a vegetarian diet] is..."
— **Neal D. Barnard, M.D., President,
The Physicians Committee For Responsible Medicine**

"Extremely useful data about health and nutrition. I appreciate this book, and look forward to using it often...."
— **Mollie Katzen, Author of *Moosewood Cookbook*,
The Enchanted Broccoli Forest, *Still Life with Menu*,
and *Pretend Soup and Other Real Recipes***

"An important and entertaining good read....Provides rational, street smart answers to all your questions."
— **Henry Spira, Coordinator,
Animal Rights International**

"This book has the answers...that will make you smile, even laugh, while you learn."
— **Karen Davis, Ph.D., President,
United Poultry Concerns, Inc.**

"An upbeat well-crafted book...full of life..."
— **William Harris, M.D.
Staff, Kaiser Permanente Honolulu Clinic**

"This book is...[a] guide for all who want the good life...."
— **Michael W. Fox, D.Sc., Ph.D., Vice President,
The Humane Society of the United States**

"A thorough explanation..."
— **Carol Wiley Lorente, Food Editor, *Vegetarian Times***

"A good and easy read..."
— **Congressman Andy Jacobs, Jr.,
U.S. House of Representatives, Washington, D.C.**

"This is an amazing book — it'll change your life, and maybe save it. Buy it, read it, give it to your friends — it's the best present they'll ever get."
—**Lewis G. Regenstein, Author of Pulitzer Prize nominated
How to Survive America the Poisoned;
Director, The Interfaith Council for
the Protection of Animals and Nature**

"A fun read! A breezy recap of the basics served up with good humor...and spiced with scores of jaw-dropping revelations.... "
— Gar Smith, Editor, *Earth Island Journal*

"[A] thoughtful collection of answers to commonly asked questions about vegetarianism...a valuable guide..."
— Lorri Bauston, President, Farm Sanctuary

"Comprehensive and user-friendly...fresh and persuasive...[with] practical tips to help the budding vegetarian..."
— Mary Margaret Cunniff, Executive Director, National Anti-Vivisection Society

"If you are not a vegetarian, you owe it to yourself to get this book."
— Cleveland Amory, Author; President, Fund For Animals; President, New England Anti-Vivisection Society

"Clear, clever, and right on time...David Gabbe entertains while he enlightens."
— Michael Klaper, M.D. Author of *Vegan Nutrition: Pure and Simple*

"Delightful...educational and entertaining..."
— Zoe Weil, Director of Education, The American Anti-Vivisection Society

"Straightforward...clear and thought-provoking..."
— Deborah Madison, Author of *The Savory Way* and *The Greens Cookbook*

"This book will save lives...."
— Priscilla Feral, President, Friends Of Animals

also by
David A. Gabbe

The Portland Super Shopper

Oregon's Coast:
A Guide to the Best Family Attractions
from Astoria to Brookings

Why Do Vegetarians Eat Like That?

Everything You Wanted To Know
(and some things you didn't)
About Vegetarianism

David A. Gabbe

Illustrations by Tony Appert

Prime Imprints, Ltd.
Eugene, Oregon

The information in this book is general and not intended to
furnish medical advice. Please consult your health care provider
for advice on any specific health problems you have.

Illustrations © Prime Imprints, Ltd., 1994

Library of Congress Card Catalog Number: 94-66410

Gabbe, David A., 1950-
    Why Do Vegetarians Eat Like That? Everything You
Wanted To Know (and some things you didn't) About
Vegetarianism / David A. Gabbe — 1st ed.

Includes bibliographical references and index.
1. Vegetarianism. 2. Nutrition. 3. Health.

ISBN 0-9640190-0-0

Prime Imprints books are available at special quantity discounts
for bulk purchases for sales promotions, premiums, fund-
raising, or educational use. For details contact: Special Sales
Director, Prime Imprints, Ltd., P.O. Box 5163, Eugene, Oregon
97405, (503) 484-5145, FAX (503) 484-5145.

Recognizing the importance of preserving both the environment
and the written word, Prime Imprints, Ltd., by policy, prints all
of its books on recycled, acid-free paper.

Printed in the United States of America

10 9 8 7 6 5 4 3 2 1

First Edition

Contents

Acknowledgements

I would first like to thank my publisher, Prime Imprints, Ltd., for seeing the promise in this book — and giving me the opportunity to write it.

For their valuable advice, I would like to thank Herb Price, Forrest Smith, and Paola Moyano.

My thanks also to Seymour Sommer for his key advice early on that I broaden the scope of the book.

Many, many people have helped with this book. I'd like to give special thanks to the staffs of the following organizations for providing information used in this book: American Anti-Vivisection Society, American Holistic Medical Association, American Holistic Veterinary Medical Association, American Vegan Society, Animal Legal Defense Fund, *Animals' Agenda*, Center for Science in the Public Interest, *Delicious! Magazine*, Earth Island Institute, EarthSave, Farm Animal Reform Movement, Farm Sanctuary, Friends of Animals, Fund for Animals, Humane Farming Association, Humane Society of the United States, Institute for Food and Development, Interfaith Council for the Protection of Animals and Nature, International Society for Animal Rights, Jews for Animal Rights, National Alliance for Animals, National Anti-Vivisection Society, *Natural Health*, North American Vegetarian Society, People for the Ethical Treatment Of Animals, Physicians Committee for Responsible Medicine, Rainforest Action Network, The Soyfoods Center, United Poultry Concerns, VEGEDINE, Vegetarian Education Network, *Vegetarian Gourmet*, Vegetarian Nutrition Dietetic Practice Group, Vegetarian Resource Group, *Vegetarian Times*, *Veggie Life*, and Youth for Environmental Sanity.

My thanks also to CJ Gabbe and Wendy Gabbe for their many suggestions regarding style.

And, of course, many thanks to all those people who asked the many questions that inspired the creation of this book.

In soliciting comments and suggestions, I sent the manuscript to a number of people around the country. I wish to express my sincere thanks to those who reviewed the manuscript and sent me their observations and criticisms. They are Sue Frederick, Dick Allgire, Kim Stallwood, George Eisman, Ingrid Newkirk, Ron Pickarski, Jennie Collura, Dr. Neal Barnard, Mollie Katzen, Henry Spira, Dr. Karen Davis, Dr. Willian Harris, Dr. Michael Fox, Deborah Madison, Carol Wiley Lorente, Congressman Andy Jacobs, Jr., Lewis Regenstein, Gar Smith, Lorri Bauston, Mary Margaret Cunniff, Cleveland Amory, Dr. Michael Klaper, Zoe Weil, and Priscilla Feral. You have all touched my heart with your generosity.

And special thanks to my mother, Esther Gabbe, who, as a young widow, single-handedly raised her three young children to be decent, caring human beings. She will ever be one of the many, great unsung heroines of our time.

Finally, I am especially grateful to my wife, Carolyn, for her understanding and support of this, and every project I've ever undertaken. Without her I could not succeed; with her I cannot fail.

Preface

After nearly twenty years of vegetarian activism — which, together with my wife, includes raising two children as vegetarians — I've come to be familiar with the questions most often asked about a vegetarian diet. And while so much is now known about the benefits of a vegetarian diet, many people still harbor numerous misconceptions about vegetarianism.

In fact, even many vegetarians don't always know how to respond to inquiries about their lifestyle. Which is really a shame. Because each question is really a wonderful opportunity to portray vegetarianism as it really is — rich in wholesome, life-giving nutrients, bursting with taste and color, devoid of environmental destruction and economic waste, and untainted by animal misery and slaughter.

So I decided to do a book that would provide short, accessible answers to basic questions about vegetarianism. A primer on the subject for newcomers, as well as a useful reference for veteran vegetarians. For simplicity, I chose a question-and-answer format — fully aware that entire books can be (and often have been) written about many of the questions I have included.

With this book, my intention is not only to clear up popular misconceptions about vegetarianism, but also to encourage readers to seek longer answers — especially by turning to works of such contemporary, renowned figures as Robbins, Lappé, Ornish, McDougall, Fox, Klaper, Barnard, Diamond, Newkirk, Null, Regan, Singer, Rifkin, Shurtleff & Aoyagi, Amory, or others I've recommended in Appendix III.

I encourage everyone to consider lending support to the many activist organizations that are laboring to make this a better world for all living creatures. And to study the arguments in favor of vegetarianism and take them to heart.

In the words of the late Nobel Prize-winning author Isaac Bashevis Singer: "To be a vegetarian is to disagree — to disagree with the course of things today. Starvation, world hunger, cruelty, waste, wars — we must make a statement against these things. Vegetarianism is my statement. And I think it's a strong one."

Chapter 1
Vegetarian Basics

I'd like to quit eating meat. Could a vegetarian diet meet all of my nutritional needs?

You bet it could. It's not only possible — it's easy — to maintain excellent health on a diet that's free of all animal flesh. In fact, our bodies have absolutely no requirement for any animal products at all. Every indispensable nutrient we need for optimal health, especially the essential amino acids, can be derived from a plant-food diet.

That may sound hard to believe at first, but there's ample evidence to justify the conclusion that vegetarianism is the most healthful diet of all! Compared to meat eaters, vegetarians have a much lower incidence of chronic ailments such as cancer, heart disease, high blood pressure, and osteoporosis.

Furthermore, studies by Dean Ornish, the renowned researcher and physician, have shown that a vegetarian diet can actually undo the damages brought on by years of meat-eating. Dr. Ornish's research has revealed that atherosclerosis (a leading cause of heart attacks and strokes) can actually be reversed by following a plant-based diet. Talk about a new lease on life!

Incidentally, people of all ages — from infants to seniors, with pregnant women and athletes thrown in, too — can follow a vegetarian diet and reap the rewards of good health. Oh, one more thing. Vegetarians live longer. That's right. Studies show that vegetarians outlive their meat-eating counterparts by a decade or more.

My vegetarian sister runs on fries, sodas, pastries, and candy bars. Even vegetarians can't live on stuff like that, can they?

Of course not. Although it's commendable that your sister has given up flesh foods, her choosing a path of poor nutrition is certainly not a prudent decision. As a junk food vegetarian, her health (and appearance) will suffer as surely as if she were following the standard meat-based American diet.

All vegetarians would be wise to heed the elementary advice of the American Dietetic Association. Namely, that a healthy, varied plant-based diet should include fresh fruits and vegetables (especially plenty of leafy greens!), whole grain products, legumes (beans, peas, and lentils), and nuts and seeds. Such a diet may also incorporate, for those wishing to have some animal products on the menu, a couple of eggs per week, and a modest amount of low-fat milk, cheese, and yogurt.

There's really nothing complicated about following a vegetarian diet. No need to mess with nutrition charts and calculators, or worry about mixing and matching vegetarian foods. Just eat as much as you wish of a variety of wholesome plant-based foods — and nature will take care of the rest.

How does a meatless diet promote good health?

By eating the right foods and by avoiding the wrong ones, vegetarians are able to boost their own body's natural striving for well-being. On the other hand, consuming a regimen of high-fat, high-protein flesh foods — like running diesel fuel through your car's gasoline engine — is a sure-fire prescription for disaster. Witness all the heart-breaking, chronic diseases afflicting meat eaters today.

It can't really be that simple, can it?

Besides saturated fat and excess protein, all meats contain varying levels of growth hormones, antibiotics, tranquilizers, stimulants, bacteria, and other toxins which have found their way into farm animals during breeding and processing. By not consuming these poisons, vegetarians are freed from the undue stress and strain placed on their immune systems.

And because they don't have to toil exhaustingly at digesting the overabundance of fat and protein in each meat dish, or to fight off all those poisons found in meat, vegetarians can use this untapped energy to maintain health and ward off disease. Yes, like falling off a log, it is that simple.

Now that's quite a statement. Do you have any proof on that?

Brace yourself. The findings are nothing short of incredible. Researchers in Germany, while doing comparative studies of white blood cell activity in vegetarian and nonvegetarian groups, discovered that the vegetarians' immune systems were stronger and had more than twice the ability of their meat-eating counterparts to destroy cancer cells. Twice! And epidemiological statistics bear those observations out. Vegetarians do have a much lower likelihood than meat eaters of falling victim to cancer.

Can organically grown meats be part of a healthy diet?

When you say "organically grown meats" you're obviously referring to farm animals that are raised without growth hormones, antibiotics, chemicalized feed, and the like. As you'll see, organic meat is no health food. There are many reasons why it should be avoided. First, let's remember that humans have absolutely no nutritional needs for meat in the diet. All the essentials can be obtained from plant-based foods. Countless studies (as well as generation upon generation of healthy vegetarians) prove it.

Second, organically grown or not, all meats, including fish and fowl, are unquestionably loaded with cholesterol and fat. Make that thick, saturated, artery-clogging fat. Is it any wonder that every few minutes a citizen of our land keels over and dies from the effects of fat-blocked arteries? Even the leanest meats have excessive, hidden fat lurking within.

Third, there's all that protein — highly-concentrated protein. That's the stuff found in the muscles of all animals. But who eats animal muscles? Well, anyone chomping on meat does. All those cuts in the grocery meat cases are muscles. And excessive protein has been fingered in countless studies as the culprit behind osteoporosis, a serious condition in which your bones lose minerals and become easily fractured.

Anything else I need to know?

Yes. All animal flesh, organically grown or not, can harbor parasites, bacteria, and a host of diseases. As soon as an animal is slaughtered, the meat begins to putrefy. And for all those countless bacteria that normally just knock around in the animal's tissues, there's no place better to be than in decaying flesh, where they thrive and multiply like mad. No wonder there are so many reported outbreaks of food poisoning. Incredibly, millions of meat eaters live their lives troubled by fatigue, diarrhea, and a flu bug they just can't seem to shake — without realizing they're actually suffering from undiagnosed food poisoning.

Other risks to human health lurk within animal flesh. As the animals are about to be slaughtered, they sense their impending dooms and react, not surprisingly, with rage, fear, and horror. Their own hormones, especially adrenalin, gush furiously throughout their bodies, flooding the tissues. After death, these abnormal levels of hormones remain in the meat and are later passed on to humans.

And then there are the toxic wastes. It's known that the heart and brain of a freshly-slaughtered animal stops functioning immediately. At the cellular level, however, that's not the case. Countless billions of cells, still momentarily nourished by contact with the just-killed animal's blood, continue their short lives and all their functions — including the production of waste materials. Normally, the living animal's circulatory system would carry off these poisonous wastes. But the animal is no longer living — its systems are shut down for good. The wastes build up, kill the cells, then remain trapped in the putrefying flesh — awaiting the trip to your dining room table.

Is "organically grown" meat a health food? Hardly. All meats, no matter how environmentally-correct they are raised, are loaded with fat, pathogens, toxins, and other waste byproducts. Avoid them like the plague.

What's this I hear about vegetarians living longer than meat eaters?

It's true. I'd like to share the results of a landmark study which may well inspire you to become a vegetarian — perhaps the single most important step that you can take to prevent going to an early grave.

Over a twenty-year period about thirty thousand adult Seventh-Day Adventists participated in a monumental inquiry into aging. Conducted by David Snowdon, Ph.D., and his associates at California's Loma Linda University, this long-term epidemiological study made a bold discovery: Vegetarians live substantially longer than their meat-eating counterparts. And, we're not talking about a piddly few years here. But a remarkable ten to fifteen years of additional living! Enough extra time to enjoy your great-grandchildren growing up.

That's just one study. Any others?

You bet. The Adventist probe was not the only one to demonstrate vegetarian longevity. Scientists investigating communities around the globe have made equally momentous discoveries.

The residents of Vilacabamba (Ecuador), who follow a largely vegetarian diet, were tested to be virtually free of heart disease, cancers, osteoporosis, obesity, and most symptoms of "old age." These people frequently live healthy and active lives beyond 100 years of age.

Similar studies were made of the Hunzans of Northern Pakistan, and of the Abkhasians, who reside near the Black Sea in the former Soviet Union. Gerontologists involved in examining these groups found vibrant, active persons who work and play well beyond the age of 80. And most who reach their 100th year remain alert and actively involved in community affairs. Again, mostly vegetarian diets were the rule here.

Yet another investigation. This one involved 100 year old men and women living in Hungary. Researchers found that these centenarians (can you guess?) were following a chiefly vegetarian diet.

Vegetarians can't live forever — but they can, as we've seen, live healthy and active lives well beyond the age where their meat-eating counterparts have already succumbed to debilitating and degenerative diseases.

Is there some miracle-working ingredient in a meatless diet that lets vegetarians live longer?

Well, if there is a single vegetarian "magic bullet" it's certainly not been spotted yet. Many nutritionists believe that it's the vegetarian diet taken as a whole, that performs such wonderworks. Let's take a look at the cold, hard facts.

Considerable evidence has been compiled showing that a plant-based diet not only contributes to vibrant health, but also greatly reduces one's risk of falling victim to most of the degenerative disorders, including cancer and heart disease — the biggest killers today. And with these life-threatening conditions held at bay, a vegetarian has greatly-improved odds of living a long and active life.

It seems only logical that if vegetarians can manage to keep killer diseases away, and to eat foods that promote optimum health, that they'd occupy the catbird seat when it comes to longevity.

What about free radicals?

I can see you've done your homework. The free radical-vegetarian diet relationship is complicated enough that entire books have been written about it. Still, let's take a quick look at this fascinating subject.

Free radicals, a vivid name that brings to mind revolutionary bomb-throwers, are highly unstable, reactive molecules that can damage every cell in the body. They're believed by many researchers to be the cause of heart disease, cancer, and premature aging. So how do you avoid them? You can't. These hazardous molecules are everywhere — they're in your body right now.

Free radicals are found in such pollutants as smog, pesticides, tobacco smoke — all the nasty places you'd expect to find damaging substances. But would you think that sunshine would also be an offender? Sunshine? That's right. As the sun's rays bathe you in a golden glow of warmth and relaxation, your skin cells are stimulated by solar energy into reacting with oxygen, creating free radicals.

Just a moment. Then why aren't we all dropping like flies on account of free radicals?

Precisely because free radicals are an inescapable menace, nature has endowed you with natural defense mechanisms. These defenders, called antioxidants, inhibit the chemical process (called oxidation) that free radicals need to conduct their destructive business. Thus, within the body, a constant battle wages as defenders hold invaders in check. As long as there is equilibrium, there's no danger. It's thought by many nutritionists that over a period of time, however, a meat-based diet so weakens the body that the free radicals gain the upper hand. And the results, which may take years to become manifest, are quite grim: coronary artery disease, cancerous tumors, and an early demise.

Now for the good news. Enter our vegetarian diet connection. It turns out that the richest source of antioxidants can be found in a plant-based diet. And by flooding their bodies with antioxidants (vegetarian eating isn't just tasty, it's medicinal!), vegetarians neutralize more free radicals and for longer periods of time than do meat eaters. And studies "prove" what we already know: Vegetarians are not only at reduced risk for most major diseases — they live longer than just about everybody.

What exactly is a vegetarian?
Do they eat chicken and fish?

Simply, a vegetarian is one who consumes no flesh foods, namely, no red meat, no fish, and no chicken. When we talk about red meat we usually are referring to beef and pork. But it also includes the flesh of calves, sheep, buffalo, deer, rabbits, and many other animals. Any food that comes by way of death or injury to an animal is steered clear of by vegetarians. So while chicken or fish may be transitional foods for those on the road to vegetarianism, these flesh foods cannot be included in a vegetarian diet.

Without question, vegetarianism has never been as popular as it is today. And while it is commendable that many people are comfortable with the "V" word, it would be a contradiction in terms to describe one who even just infrequently eats flesh foods as a "part-time vegetarian" or "semi-vegetarian." To consider occasionally eating meat as "vegetarian" would disregard twenty-five centuries of authentic vegetarian tradition. As with pregnancy, you either are or you aren't.

I've heard the terms "pesco" and "pollo" used in reference to vegetarians. What do they mean?

Some people jokingly refer to "vegetarians" who eat fish as pesco-vegetarians and those who eat chicken as pollo-vegetarians (in Spanish, "pescado" means fish, and "pollo" means chicken). But these odd designations must be looked at as tongue-in-cheek, since those who eat any animal flesh are not vegetarians.

Perhaps what these terms do signify is that vegetarianism has become so acceptable to the public that many people wish to openly affiliate with it. And though the terms pesco and pollo-vegetarians are nothing more than oxymorons, they could, in a broader sense, be the labels used by many who consider themselves in transition to vegetarianism.

Not all vegetarians eat eggs and dairy products. How many different vegetarian diets are there?

Vegetarians all agree on one thing: Flesh foods are not part of a vegetarian diet. But as you've observed, vegetarians do differ on whether to consume animal foods like milk, cheese, eggs, and honey. To better understand vegetarianism, it might be useful to know that there are two major "types" of vegetarians: **ovo-lacto** vegetarians and **vegans** (also known as "pure" or "strict" vegetarians).

Ovo-lacto vegetarians make up the bulk of those following a vegetarian diet. Since "ovo" comes from the Latin for egg, and "lacto" for milk, it's easy to see that ovo-lacto vegetarians include dairy products and eggs (and honey, too) in their diets. For many people, ovo-lacto vegetarianism is but a stepping-stone, a transition diet on the path to the purest form of vegetarianism — veganism.

Veganism is often referred to as "strict" vegetarianism because its adherents live exclusively on a plant-based diet. Vegans (pronounced vee-guns) avoid all dairy products, eggs, honey, lard, gelatin, and any other food of animal origin. They also make every effort to avoid hidden animal by-products that typically pop up in cosmetics, oils, clothing, household goods, and other items.

It's often asked whether a vegan can be adequately nourished on such "limited" fare. The answer is an unqualified yes. Studies suggest that the strict vegetarian diet is ideal for optimum well-being and for maintaining a healthy heart and circulatory system.

And beyond these two major varieties of vegetarianism, there are two additional levels within levels. There are some vegetarians who add eggs, but not dairy products, to their diets. Recalling our earlier introduction to Latin, we can see why they're called ovo-vegetarians. And those vegetarians who exclude eggs, but eat dairy products, are known as lacto-vegetarians

Do most people who become vegetarians do so for health reasons?

Yes, that's right. Studies show that a majority of those choosing a vegetarian diet do so out of concern for their health. They reject animal flesh because of the growth hormones and antibiotics routinely fed farm animals, as well as the various toxins, harmful bacteria, and chemicals found in all flesh foods.

Other health-minded individuals become vegetarians because of their objection to the high-fat, high-cholesterol content of meat, poultry, and fish. As you've undoubtedly heard, numerous studies link the consumption of these fats and cholesterol with the onset of heart disease, cancer, and other degenerative diseases.

Although concern for personal health is the prime motivation for adopting a vegetarian diet, there are other compelling reasons for doing so.

What are those?

The tremendous environmental destruction and waste of resources attributed to the production of meat are serious issues that cry out for a vegetarian solution. Tropical rainforests, so important to world climate stability, are being cut down at staggering rates in order to provide grazing land for vast herds of cattle. These animals are later turned into cheap beef for the fast food industry.

In addition, the raising of livestock consumes shocking amounts of fresh water — accounting for half of all the water consumed in America. Feedlots the size of small cities dot the landscape, contributing the majority of all the toxic chemicals found in our fresh water resources. And that's not all. Countless millions of gallons of fuel must be burned to operate the equipment that feeds, houses, transports, and processes the billions of farm animals slaughtered each year.

And while millions of people, many of them children, go hungry or starve to death around the world, the production of meat requires that animals be fed 15 pounds of high-protein beans and grains merely to produce one pound of edible meat. That's a loss of no less than 14 pounds of nourishing food for each pound of meat produced. This shameful and inefficient practice wastes mountains of edible foodstuffs that otherwise could be better used to end world hunger and meet the needs of the planet's increasing population for millenia to come.

An argument that reaches to the depths of humanity makes the case that since humans have no known nutritional requirement for eating meat, unnecessary suffering and death are inflicted on animals merely to satisfy your taste buds. With an abundance of plant-based foods, there's no justifiable reason to kill animals for food. And while animals may not merit the protection of the Bill of Rights, don't they at least have the "right" to be left alone?

We've covered the primary reasons for becoming a vegetarian. However, there's another motivation — although less profound and heartfelt than the others — that can be added. It has to do with aesthetics, or taste. One day, a meat eater sees the light, making the connection that the juicy bit of steak being chewed is really muscle tissue, fat, and blood taken from the corpse of an animal. It's a disgusting realization. One that's usually enough to kill the appetite for meat forever.

Why do strict vegetarians avoid milk and eggs? After all, animals aren't killed for these products.

Strict vegetarians, better known as vegans, refrain from these animal foods for several reasons. Some vegetarians are allergic to both milk and egg whites and simply choose to give up these products without further ado. Nothing philosophical or ethical about it.

Other vegetarians, concerned about their health, swear off dairy products and eggs because these things are highly concentrated sources of growth hormones, antibiotics, and chemicals — hazardous substances routinely fed to farm animals. And these foods may also harbor salmonella (causes food poisoning) and other virulent bacteria.

And there's yet another reason why vegans choose to reject all foods of animal origin. Namely, because they believe the exploitation of animals to be morally wrong. Admittedly, there's no direct killing of cows and chickens in the production of milk and eggs. But vegans feel that eating these products is tantamount to supporting industries that brutally exploit animals in horrible factory-farm settings. And once their short, productive lives have been deemed to be of no further value, cows and chickens are dispatched to the slaughterhouse.

In adopting a vegetarian diet, is it better to do it quickly, or bit by bit?

There's no right answer. Some people prefer to make the change to vegetarianism overnight (going "cold turkey"), while others do it gradually — taking weeks, months, or even years. There's no medical evidence favoring one approach over the other. Regardless of which way you do it, adopting a meatless diet is a bold step which can give your system quite a little jolt.

Most aspiring vegetarians choose to make the change a little at a time. This is an advantageous approach as it makes it easier for the body to acclimate itself to the new healthful diet. For example, they immediately stop eating red meat but continue with fish and fowl on the menu. When they feel adjusted to this change, they proceed to drop birds from the diet, but not seafood, yet. Again, after getting used to things, they're ready to move on, to say goodbye to fish — and hello to vegetarianism.

Yet another gradual approach involves following your regular fare of flesh foods on the first and third weeks of each month; and vegetarian foods on the second and fourth weeks. After a few months, you drop the flesh food weeks — and voilà, you're a vegetarian.

Making the change a little at a time seems to work out well for most converts to vegetarianism. You miss meat less and less when it's gradually dropped from the diet.

As long as you take on a vegetarian diet slowly there shouldn't be any side effects, right?

Brace yourself for one heck of an enormous side effect. In practically no time at all, you'll start feeling better than you've ever felt before. But, in the first few days or weeks some people experience a bit of discomfort.

Why? Because if you've eaten refined foods your whole life (and remember, meat has no fiber) you've got a digestive system that's unfamiliar with all the fiber and bulk found in a wholesome plant-based diet. And fiber causes gas. Until your colon has enlarged to handle the new supply of gas, there may be some cramping.

Many new vegetarians report experiencing the following effects:

• **Abundant energy** (since vegetarian foods are easier to digest than meats, the digestive system doesn't have to work as hard, providing more freed-up energy for greater zip and oomph!);

• **weight loss** (since vegetarian diets are lower in fat and calories than flesh foods, the pounds seem to melt away almost effortlessly);

• **enhanced mental clarity** (the cerebral processes are humming without all the animal fat clogging up the

arteries that carry blood to the brain); and
- **sweeter breath and body odor** (what else should you expect without those nasty meat-derived toxins and wastes to excrete through your skin and mouth?).

If I quit meat, it'll be all at once. Really, how hard on the body is a sudden switch to vegetarianism?

For most people it's not hard at all. Sure, the gradual approach to a vegetarian diet minimizes any jolt the body feels, but most of those who quit flesh foods cold turkey don't have any problems, either. No matter what approach you take, you may experience some temporary gas or cramping because of the introduction of fiber into a diet that was previously devoid of it. But the body quickly adjusts.

The major difference between a sudden approach and a gradual one has to do with the body's internal cleansing process. In every body, meat eater and vegetarian alike, the clean up crews are always at work eliminating pollutants. But in meat eaters, the body is overloaded with toxins, making the clean up process an ineffective and futile act. And this concentration of toxic substances plays a key role in the development of degenerative disease.

However, when a vegetarian diet is adopted, the heavy flow of meat-derived toxins (growth hormones, antibiotics, pesticides, stimulants, bacteria, and wastes) into the body is abruptly halted. This cessation allows the internal cleaners to get to work — and they do so with a vengeance. Enormous amounts of locked-up toxins are wrenched loose and dumped into the blood for removal from the body. It can be quite a kick in the keister.

For this reason some people who jump into a vegetarian diet overnight may suffer unpleasant, but temporary, side effects like headaches, foul breath and body odor, pimples, and a number of other minor complaints — all due to the rapid elimination of years of accumulated waste.

Although it may be difficult to feel good about these manifestations, they're actually signs that the vegetarian diet is in sync with the body's natural desire to keep itself clean — an important function for good health and longevity. Ironically, some people interpret these side effects as evidence that a meatless diet is harming them. They give up and return to their unwholesome flesh food diets. A tragic misunderstanding.

Incidentally, those who become vegetarians little by little probably wouldn't even notice any of these unpleasant housecleaning effects, since the cleansing process is so gradual.

I've heard that when you stop eating meat you're hungry all the time. Is that true?

Initially, many new vegetarians are indeed surprised to discover that they're habitually hungry. That's because a plant-based diet is high in carbohydrates and low in fat. These are important factors that permit the digestive system to function at optimal efficiency in hustling the food along. Fat, a major component of meat, just sits in the stomach, taking forever to move out.

But the novice vegetarian's stomach may start rumbling long before the next regularly scheduled mealtime. What to do about this? Simple. Just eat bigger meals, making sure you choose from a wide variety of wholesome, vegetarian foods. Or why not just eat healthful, natural snacks between meals? Either approach should do the trick. In time, you adjust and learn to consume just the right amount of calories you need to avoid those irksome hunger pangs. But be prepared to experience a permanent feeling of lightness — a perception unknown to those who devour animal flesh.

Doesn't becoming a vegetarian mean a lifetime of eating mostly bean curds and brown rice?

Hardly. Many people have yet to catch on that a vegetarian diet offers an incredible richness and diversity limited only by the imagination of the cook. And in the past few years there's been a mushrooming of exceptional vegetarian cookbooks to guide new vegetarians to many exciting culinary adventures. There are so many appetizing foods to select from that you'll quickly forget about all those tasteless flesh foods that require heaps of flavoring to be palatable.

In fact, if vegetarians have a problem, it's having too much to choose from. There's so much finger-lickin' good vegetarian food, and oh, so little time. A first visit to a health food store should be quite an education as to the abundance of meatless choices now available. You'll find excellent, high-protein meat substitutes like tofu and tempeh that can be prepared in countless ways. If you're looking for convenience foods, you'll find vegetarian burgers and hot dogs, as well as meatless "bacon," "bologna," and "cold cuts." They look and taste so "real" that many vegetarians won't touch them.

Feel like meatloaf? Forget it. Try a lentil loaf instead. And lasagne, with tofu and soy cheese, makes a nutritious alternative to fat-laden flesh foods. Some other vegetarian foods you may encounter on your health food store tour include: soy milk, azuki beans, brewer's yeast, chickpeas, quinoa, miso, basmati rice, buckwheat, shoyu, and ...

Whoa, hold on. I don't want those strange things. Can't you live on simple vegetarian foods found at the grocery store?

Of course you can. Shopping for vegetarian foods need never pose a problem. Supermarkets can provide all the fruits, vegetables, whole grain products, beans, peas, nuts, and seeds needed to thrive on a vegetarian diet.

Most vegetarians have no trouble whatsoever shopping for such "exotic," meatless foods, like spaghetti, bean burritos, corn flakes, cottage cheese, eggs, pancake mix, macaroni and cheese, peanut butter and jelly, cheese pizza with vegetable toppings, and a warehouse more.

Doesn't the term "vegetarian" really mean "vegetable-eater"?

Not at all. Perhaps few other words in the English language have been so misunderstood as "vegetarian." Most people, and that includes many a dictionary editor, erroneously think the term "vegetarian" derives from vegetable. It does not. "Vegetarian" comes from the Latin **vegetus**, which means "whole, energetic, and full of life." Thus, the ancient Romans used the expression "homo vegetus" to mean a person full of vim and vigor.

"Vegetarian" was specifically coined by the founders of the British Vegetarian Society in the mid-19th century to make a critical statement. Namely, that they were going to lead lives that were physically and spiritually pure.

Regrettably, all too many nutrition specialists make the mistake of viewing vegetarians as emaciated, vegetable-eating creatures in need of real food (make that meat). Ain't so. And this naive view, partly based on a misreading of what "vegetarian" really means, has led to many false arguments against vegetarianism. Which is such a travesty, considering that countless studies have concluded that vegetarians are far healthier than meat eaters.

Isn't vegetarianism nothing but a fad diet supported by a relatively small number of radicals and food extremists?

That couldn't be further from the truth. Vegetarians, in one shape or another, have been around since the dawn of man (and woman!). Scientists conclude that long before the advent of "modern" vegetarianism some 25 centuries ago, our earliest ancestors were vegetarians who ate flesh foods only in periods of dire emergency. With the onset of the Ice Age, these early men and women were deprived of their natural diet of nuts, berries, fruits, and vegetables. They resorted to animal flesh as the only means of survival.

Historically, vegetarianism can be traced to the teachings of the Greek philosopher Pythagoras who lived six hundred years before Christ. Pythagoras believed that a diet free of animal flesh was not only compassionate and ecological, but also promoted good physical and mental health. Sound familiar? These are notions still espoused by vegetarians everywhere.

By the way, for those who remember their geometry, Pythagoras was the fellow who originated that memorable statement about right triangles: "The hypotenuse squared is equal to the sum of the squares of the other two sides." Fortunately, we need go no further into it.

Up until the 19th century, followers of Pythagoras' meatless diet were known as Pythagoreans. Why not "vegetarians"? Because the term "vegetarian" wasn't coined until the 1840's, when the British Vegetarian Society first set up shop.

And does vegetarianism have any famous followers? You bet! Some of the world's greatest scientists, artists, writers, and leaders were vegetarians: Henry David Thoreau, Louisa May Alcott, Plato, Socrates, Sir Isaac Newton, Gandhi, Leonardo da Vinci, Charles Darwin, Buddha, Leo Tolstoy, Ralph Waldo Emerson, Albert Schweitzer, Voltaire, George Bernard Shaw, Isaac Bashevis Singer, Clara Barton, Cesar Chavez, Thomas Edison, Scott Nearing, Rousseau, Mary Wollstonecraft Shelley, Upton Sinclair, H.G. Wells, and Albert Einstein.

Contemporary vegetarians include:

TV and Film: Casey Kasem, Fred "Mr." Rogers, Christie Brinkley, John Tesh, John Corbett, Dennis Weaver, Steve Martin, Kim Basinger, Dick Gregory, Susan St. James, Cloris Leachman, Madonna, Bob Barker, Lindsay Wagner, Peter Falk, Hayley Mills, Meredith Baxter, Ellen Burstyn, Kirk Cameron, Cicely Tyson, Elvira, Sara Gilbert, Elliot Gould, Doug Henning, Peggy Lipton, Marina Sirtis, Dustin Hoffman, Phylicia Rashad, Tracy Pollan, Kevin Nealon, and Donna Mills.

Music: Paul and Linda McCartney, k.d. lang, Henry Blomstedt (conductor), David Bowie, Olivia Newton-John, Raffi, Rick Springfield, Chrissie Hynde (Pretenders), Bryan Adams, Anthony Kiedes (Red Hot Chili Peppers), Joe Elliott and Phil Collen (Def Leppard), Jerry Garcia (Grateful Dead), Natalie Merchant, Michael Stipe (R.E.M.), and Eddie Vedder (Pearl Jam).

Athletics: Henry Aaron (pro baseball), Murray Rose (Olympic swimmer), Tony La Russa (pro baseball), Billie Jean King (tennis), Andreas Cahling (Mr. International/body builder), Marv Levy (pro football), Surya Bonaly (Olympic ice-skater), Al Oerter (Olympic discus thrower), Martina Navratilova (tennis), Paavo Nurmi (Olympic runner), Roger Brown (pro football), Killer Kowalski (pro wrestler), Leroy Burrell (Olympic track), Peter Burwash (Davis cup winner/tennis), Chris Campbell (Olympic wrestler), Carl Lewis (Olympic runner), Edwin Moses (Olympic track), and Bill Pearl (Mr. Universe/body builder).

Writing: Colman McCarthy, Jeremy Rifkin, Frances Moore Lappé, Cleveland Amory, Mollie Katzen, Deborah Madison, William Shurtleff, Akiko Aoyagi, Lorna Sass, Robert James Waller, Brigid Brophy, Marilyn and Harvey Diamond, Gary Null, John Robbins, Keith Akers, Michael Medved, Helen Nearing, Tom Regan, Corydon Ireland, and Chef Ron Pickarski.

Others: U.S. Representative Andrew Jacobs, Henry Heimlich, M.D., T. Colin Campbell, Ph.D., Dean Ornish, M.D., John McDougall, M.D., Michael Klaper, M.D., Neal Barnard, M.D., Steven Jobs, Alex Hershaft, Ingrid Newkirk, Jeffrey Bland, Ph.D., Michael Fox, Ph.D., Freya and Jay Dinshah, Reed Mangels, Ph.D., R.D., Suzanne Havala, M.S., R.D., Charles Stahler, Debra Wasserman, Alex Pacheco, William C. Roberts, M.D., and countless others.

But wasn't Hitler a vegetarian, too?

Adolph Hitler was a lot of things, but being a vegetarian wasn't one of them. The popular legend that Hitler was a vegetarian probably originated with aides who were completely unfamiliar with the tenets of vegetarianism.

Arguably, the German Fuehrer generally excluded meat and fish from his diet. He subsisted for the most part on an unwholesome, sugary diet of cream cakes, candies, pastries, sugared fruits, chocolates, and sugar-laden coffee and tea. (A sweet tooth to match his awesome ego!) But Hitler's special fondness for Bavarian sausages and caviar assuredly would have kept him out of the German Vegetarian Society. Of course, Hitler needn't have felt snubbed by any vegetarian organizations. When he came to power, he banned all vegetarian groups and had their leaders thrown into concentration camps.

Too bad for Hitler. He certainly could've benefitted from a wholesome, vegetarian diet. As an adult, Hitler continually suffered from severe gastric and intestinal disturbances. These included bouts of excessive flatulence — an irksome and embarrassing condition for anyone, let alone for the iron-fisted ruler of Nazi Germany.

Chapter 2

Nutrition and Health

Without meat, how do vegetarians manage to get enough protein?

Of all the questions vegetarians get asked, this one seems to top the list. And that's because Americans have a national hang-up about getting enough protein. So the "radical" notion of dropping meat from the diet must surely sound like a death sentence.

Rest assured. Vegetarians have no trouble whatsoever meeting their protein needs. In fact, numerous studies point out that vegetarians actually gobble up at least two times the Recommended Dietary Allowance (RDA) for protein. That's right. Twice as much as they need. Without meat? But how? Because just about every bean, nut, grain, and vegetable is chock full of protein. Even most fruits are modestly endowed with protein. Protein, protein — everywhere protein.

By eating a variety of unrefined, plant-based foods, vegetarians have little to be concerned about, nutritionally speaking, that is. Of course, there's always death and taxes.

But aren't plant proteins less nutritious than meat proteins?

Don't believe that for a moment. For the past forty years, the meat and dairy lobbyists have mounted a masterful public relations campaign to convince the American people that the only nourishing proteins come from — surprise! — meat and dairy products.

Due in great measure to meat and dairy industry financial support, the standard nutrition books classified meat proteins as "first class," while plant proteins were hustled off the stage as inferior "second class" proteins. And until not too long ago, this gross inaccuracy rested comfortably in the public mind.

Fortunately, to the delight of those who both pursue truth and avoid meat, scientists have recently disproved the notion that plant proteins are inferior to meat proteins. Plant proteins have been found to be as life-sustaining as meat proteins — but without the dangers inherent in meat, such as saturated fat, cholesterol, hormones, antibiotics, bacteria, and other toxins.

And as if all those nasty residues weren't enough to sound the death knell for meat-eating, we've come to learn that meat proteins contain high amounts of sulfur. This element has been indicted for its role in causing the body to lose calcium — leading eventually to a serious condition of brittle bones.

Let's back up. Aren't plant proteins "incomplete" because they're missing some amino acids?

I'm glad you asked that. First, let's deal with the charge that plant proteins are somehow "incomplete." That distorted idea goes back to the early part of this century when it was first theorized that meat proteins were "complete" because they contained all the necessary amino acids. On the other hand, plant proteins were declared to be "incomplete" since it was thought that they lacked certain amino acids.

Researchers now know that plant proteins contain all the essential amino acids. That's right — all. Every fruit, vegetable, bean, and grain has complete protein. (And doubting Thomases may verify that by referring to any food chart that shows amino acid food content.) Incredibly, some nutritionists still perpetuate the old myth about plant proteins being incomplete.

To prove a point, you could get all the protein and essential amino acids you need each day by simply eating only one food. That's right — one food. Of course, you'd have to eat a heap of this single food to do so. For example, it would take about nine cups of cooked brown rice or eight large potatoes or one and a quarter pounds of tofu to obtain the recommended dietary allowances for protein and essential amino acids.

Yet a healthful diet is much more than merely protein and amino acids. A regimen composed of one food does not supply the many other nutrients required for excellent health. For that reason, it would be hard to find a responsible dietitian who'd recommend such limited fare in lieu of a varied, wholefoods diet.

What are amino acids, anyway?

Amino acids are the chemical substances that make up all protein. Whether it be animal protein, plant protein, or a chunk of your hide, they're all composed of about two dozen amino acids.

The human body needs amino acids, often described as "building blocks," to grow and maintain healthy bones, cells, tissues, and organs. Most of these building blocks are already found in your body since your internal factories make them regularly. But eight amino acids cannot be manufactured, and must be obtained from the food you eat. These eight have become known as the "essential" amino acids.

I should point out something here. Your body doesn't make protein by simply eating protein. That's right. You've got to break down the protein you eat into amino acids. Then, and only then, can your body reassemble the pieces into protein it can use. Think of an amino acid as you would a link of a gold chain. A gold chain (protein) is made up of numerous, small gold links (amino acids) all hooked together. When you eat a meal, your digestive juices break down the proteins into amino acids — like taking apart the gold chain by opening each link, until the chain has been transformed into piles of individual links.

This is where the body creates its magic. Those stacks of amino acid building blocks are then seized over by the body's construction crew and strung together in all sorts of shapes and sizes — making new chains of proteins that are necessary for a host of life-sustaining bodily functions.

If plant proteins are complete, why do vegetarians have to "mix and match" their proteins at each meal?

Good question. Okay, it's been noted that every plant protein contains all the essential amino acids. But for your body to make optimal use of these proteins, the amino acids must not only all be present and accounted for, they must also be there in just the right proportion. However, plant-based foods, when taken alone (i.e. rice or pinto beans or broccoli or wheat or almonds, etc.), do not contain all the essential amino acids in the appropriate proportion.

That said, it would seem that plant proteins, as long argued by the meat and dairy lobbyists, are inferior sources of protein. But that's a bum rap — as demonstrated by Frances Moore Lappé in her powerfully moving book, *Diet for a Small Planet*. Written in 1971, that landmark work unveiled the idea of mixing and matching plant proteins to make them "complete" and useful for the body. The author called this process "protein complementing."

Protein complementing showed that vegetarians could mix and match plant proteins to create amino acid combinations in just the right proportions. These assembled plant proteins were shown to be even superior to meat proteins. For example, if you combined rice, which is low in certain amino acids, with beans, which are high in these same certain amino acids, the combination yielded a protein that was ideal for superior health.

But in trying to be above criticism from the nutrition experts, Lappé made this whole business of protein complementing a frightful, complicated affair. Precise grain and bean combinations were required at the same meal in order to ward off protein malnutrition. Her book was full of graphs, diagrams, charts, measurements, complex formulas — a veritable blueprint that was just way too much for most people.

However, years later, Lappé admitted she'd erred in making it seem that so much care had to go into mixing and matching proteins. Researchers have long since concluded, that while protein complementing is necessary, the whole process is easy as pie. All a vegetarian has to do to insure getting the highest quality protein is to eat a variety of unrefined grains, legumes, nuts and seeds, fruits, and vegetables **throughout the day**, not necessarily at each meal. The body is then able to do its own mixing and matching, creating complete proteins for use in a myriad of important functions.

How much protein do we need each day?

Who'd think that such an innocent question was so full of controversy? Yet sadly, while most Americans are wolfing down far more protein than they need, our nation's nutrition policy makers continue to ignore the dangers of eating excessive protein.

Okay, so how much protein does a person need? There is a consensus among the experts that adults should be taking in about as much protein as they're losing each day. Losing protein? How's that? It's happening right now. In your body, cells are dying all the time. While most of the deceased are recycled into new proteins, a small portion is lost for good.

And other miniscule amounts of protein are converted

to sugar and burned for energy. Yet more protein, albeit itsy-bitsy quantities, are lost each time you urinate, make a bowel movement, sweat, bleed, and cut your hair or nails. You're also leaving behind minute heaps of sloughed-off skin (protein) wherever you go.

While it seems as if you're hemorrhaging protein, it's really not that bad. Your total daily protein loss comes to — get this — less than an ounce. That's right, you could stuff it in an envelope and mail it for the price of one first-class stamp. No extra postage required.

Doesn't that mean you only need an ounce of protein each day?

Bingo. And doesn't that sound reasonable? Replace only what's lost and perhaps add just a scant extra bit, to top off the tank. As we've noted, many experts agree that the "in" equals "out" formula is ideal for optimal health.

So why on earth does the typical American meat eater consume nearly four times the amount of protein that's needed? We lose an ounce a day, but most meat eaters eat over three and one-half ounces of pure protein! Even the Recommended Dietary Allowance (RDA) for protein advises adults to consume at most around two ounces of pure protein daily. And that conservative recommendation is much more than you need.

Let's get a second opinion. The World Health Organization, an agency of the United Nations, recommends that adults take in one and three-quarters ounces of pure protein each day. That's still too much (remember you only lose an ounce a day), but at least it's closer to what's best for you.

Let's stop for a moment and put all this into perspective. While there's protein to be found in virtually every food, no single food is 100 percent protein. By the way, protein is measured in tiny units called grams. One ounce can hold about thirty grams. So the RDA for protein, two ounces, equals about 60 grams.

Without dumping a food chart on you, let's take a peek at how much protein is hiding in food. One cup (eight ounces) of cooked beans will provide nearly 15 grams of protein (about one-fourth of the daily RDA recommendation). One cup of cooked vegetables will give you close to five grams of protein, while one cup of cooked grains also yields about five grams. Four ounces of tofu (the typical "meat and potatoes" of vegetarianism) contain around 12 grams of protein. And two tablespoons of peanut butter hold roughly eight grams.

You can see by these figures that if you eat eight ounces of cooked beans you'll pick up 15 grams of protein, or about one-half ounce of pure protein. Again, while you lose about one ounce of pure protein each day, the daily RDA calls for two ounces of pure protein. Obviously, a vegetarian eating a varied, wholefoods diet will have no problem getting enough protein.

What's so bad about eating a little extra protein each day?

If only it were just a "little" it might not be so terrible. But as you've seen, meat eaters consume an astonishing amount of extra protein each day — three to four (and often more) times the amount actually needed. And there's plenty bad about their doing so.

Even the Recommended Dietary Allowance (RDA) "merely" doubles the actual amount of protein you need each day. So meat eaters are eating twice as much (at least) as the RDA suggests, which itself is a doubling of a person's actual daily protein requirements.

So what's the downside to all this extra protein? Well, eating more protein than necessary makes the body struggle to rid itself of the glut. Particularly, the liver and kidneys are greatly taxed from having to remove the excessive protein from the body. What the body cannot use, must be broken down and eliminated.

Furthermore, eating high-protein flesh foods causes a sudden, steep rise in the amount of amino acids entering the blood. This is a potentially dangerous situation. Fortunately, the body recognizes this imbalance and remedies it by pumping calcium (to neutralize the acids) into the blood. It works. The blood pH level returns to normal and the crisis defused — that is, until the next meat meal when the scene is replayed: the blood becomes acidic, and the body sends in the calcium. But, where is your body getting all that calcium to douse the blood each time you eat flesh foods?

From the bones, unfortunately. Your body actually dissolves bone to provide the critical calcium. Ideally, you'd expect the body to reabsorb the calcium used to neutralize the excess acid, and return it to the bones. And that would avoid any bone calcium loss. But this can't happen, because animal protein is high in sulfur, which prevents the kidneys from reabsorbing the calcium. Thus, calcium is lost, and the bones slowly become brittle and subject to fractures. Osteoporosis is not far off.

What's more, both the liver and kidneys work at a feverish rate to tear down and eliminate the profusion of amino acids that surges through the blood following a meat meal. Over a period of time, as a result of their grueling efforts, the liver and kidneys dilate and become less efficient. With these major organs functioning at less than optimal capacity, your chances of falling prey to any number of serious illnesses increase.

What can you do about this? Lots. Reduce your protein intake to an amount no greater than that suggested by the RDA recommendations. And switch to plant proteins. They're naturally lower in protein than meat, and are much easier on the body

"Experts conclude that vegetarians who eat a variety of whole grains, beans, nuts, seeds, fruits, and vegetables get all the protein they need."

How do vegetarians actually know they're getting enough protein?

Nutritionists point out that a protein deficiency is not likely to be found in those who eat a variety of unrefined grains, beans, nuts and seeds, fruits, and vegetables. As long as vegetarians gobble down enough of these foods to avoid hunger and maintain ideal body weight, they're getting all the protein (and maybe even a bit more) that they need.

Besides, if you really were protein deficient, you'd know it. You'd be a bedridden wreck, always the victim of one illness or another, and far too weak to even stand up. Among other things, your doctor would tell you that your liver wasn't working anymore. And without a liver — don't ask. And you've seen those grim images on the evening news of starving children in Africa, with their bloated stomachs and fly-infested sores. That's protein deficiency. It's not an affliction from which vegetarians suffer.

Actually, it would be practically impossible to design a varied plant-based diet that would be so low in protein as to cause such terrible deficiency symptoms.

As long as you're keeping your weight up, aren't you automatically getting enough protein?

That's true if you're on a varied, vegetarian diet. But that's not the case if you're a junk food eater getting nearly all your nourishment from fast food franchises and convenience food marts. Although such a nutritional disaster could well provide all the calories you need to maintain your weight and keep you free of hunger, it would not supply you with adequate protein. And that's how in the wealthiest nation on earth there can be tens of millions of people subsisting in various stages of malnutrition.

How can this happen? When you get most of your calories from fat, sugar, and refined flours — all of which are minimal protein sources — you effectively shut out the protein (and other vital nutrients!) that your life depends on.

You know the "foods" I'm talking about. White bread,

cookies, cakes, pastries, candy, french fries, chips, soft drinks, alcoholic beverages, greasy salad dressings, jams and jellies, lavish desserts — all examples of high-calorie, low-protein foods that use up all your daily calories without providing adequate protein. Clearly, such a regimen cannot support first-rate health. And it's especially tragic for young people who, at that important stage of life, are growing and adding muscle mass. It's not the time for them to be nutritionally shortchanged.

Are there any cases in which vegetarians should actually eat more protein than usual?

Yes, there are. Whenever the body requires more protein, that need must be met. For example, growing children, pregnant women, and women who are breastfeeding, all have needs for extra protein. Also, adults and children recovering from surgery and certain serious illnesses (or severe burns) must have more protein than usual to replace lost or damaged tissue.

But how much extra protein should you consume in such particular situations? Many nutritionists feel that the amount of additional protein required at these special times may not be all that much greater than your regular protein needs. Perhaps this can be put into perspective by focusing on pregnancy, for example.

Reed Mangels, Ph.D., R.D., indicates in *Simply Vegan* (a work Mangels co-authored with Debra Wasserman), that a mere 20 percent increase in the Recommended Dietary Allowance of protein for women is sufficient during pregnancy. Furthermore, Mangels advises that a vegetarian diet that is varied and full of excellent protein sources such as soy products, beans, and grains will provide the extra protein boost pregnant women need.

Are strict vegetarians who get no vitamin B12 in danger of developing irreversible nerve damage?

Aside from protein, many of those adopting a vegetarian diet worry about picking up enough vitamin B12. Theoretically, vegetarians who shun dairy foods and eggs, could come up short in B12, as plants are not a source of this essential nutrient.

And the medical books are not hesitant to declare that the lack of B12 is the cause of numerous disorders, including pernicious anemia and degeneration of the nervous system. Even many respected nutrition experts warn vegetarians not to abstain from milk and eggs.

But is there anything to worry about? Well, let me put it this way. Vegans (vegetarians who eat plant foods only) are nearly as likely to become B12 deficient as you are of catching sight of a herd of unicorns. Worldwide, of the millions of practicing vegans, only a small number of cases of B12 deficiency have ever been reported. How many? Less than a dozen.

Which should make us wonder. In view of their not getting B12 from animal products, why aren't the vast majority of vegans coming down with deficiency diseases?

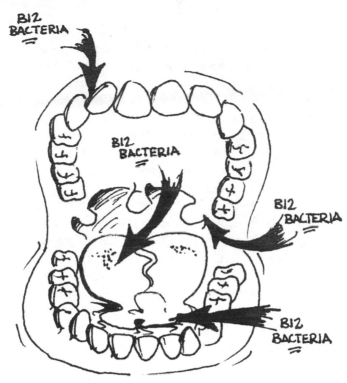

Why aren't they?

Vitamin B12, or more precisely the bacteria that actually produce the nutrient, are literally everywhere. These microorganisms are found in the intestinal tracts of animals and in the soil where they manufacture B12 as a byproduct of breaking down fiber. Neither plants nor animals, as a matter of fact, make B12. Only the bacteria themselves have the ability to make this life-sustaining element.

These B12-producing bacteria also appear, of all places, in your mouth. They're found around your teeth and gums, in your saliva, in the folds of your tongue, and in the nooks and crannies of your tonsils. In addition, these micro-manufacturers have been found in the human upper respiratory passages and in the small intestine.

Vitamin B12 has also been detected in tap water; and sporadically in and around various vegetables that have come from plots of land fertilized with manure. Thus, small but significant amounts of B12 might be riding along these vegetables in minute particles of soil.

Although these amounts of B12 are extremely small, the human requirement for this nutrient is so incredibly tiny that vegans may well be absorbing the little they need from these variant sources.

Of course, there is some controversy whether people are truly able to utilize any B12 not derived from meat, dairy, or eggs. But if not for the B12 bacteria within their bodies (and the B12 from the other aforementioned sources) how would you explain the near total-lack of B12 deficiency cases in millions of vegans who shun all animal products?

How much vitamin B12 do you need, anyway?

You require such a miniscule amount that it's measured in micrograms (mcg), or millionths of a gram. Numerous studies report that an adult does quite well on varying amounts of B12 that range from a high of .75 mcg to a low of .1 mcg per day.

On the other hand, the Recommended Dietary Allowance (RDA) for B12 is three micrograms per day. As you can see, this recommendation allows a generous built-in safety margin that at least quadruples your daily requirement as determined by the studies.

Do you remember those B12-producing bacteria that dwell in your mouth and gut? Well, they produce up to .5

mcg of B12 each day. According to many researchers, this is all you need. Furthermore, not only can the body efficiently make do with so little, it's also able to recycle B12, using its stockpile again and again.

Since we know that the body appears to have an internal B12 "production facility," does a vegan have to worry about deficiencies any more?

You've seen that the body requires but a smidgen of B12. And it seems that bacteria in the mouth and small intestine are able to produce enough of the nutrient to satisfy your needs. Yet, in spite of this, a prudent person should not rely on that source alone for the small, but critical, dose of B12. Here's why.

Although it's amazingly rare, a B12 deficiency can cause severe, irreversible damage to the nervous system. Other symptoms include the loss of sensation in the limbs, impaired memory, and the loss of balance.

Since the measure to prevent a B12 deficiency is easy and without danger, it's better to be safe than sorry. Therefore, vegetarians who consume no animal products whatsoever, would be wise to supplement their diets with vitamin B12 tablets in accords with the RDA recommendations of three mcg. each day.

Most dieticians advise vegans to take these B12 supplements at least three times a week. By reading the label, you should be able to find B12 tablets that contain at least three mcg, and which are made from non-animal sources.

I don't like vitamin pills. I've heard that sea vegetables and fermented foods contain vitamin B12. Is that true?

I'm afraid not. Some time ago it was believed that various sea vegetables, such as kombu and wakame, as well as fermented soyfoods, like tempeh and miso, were high in B12 content. Alas, recent studies have demonstrated that these products are not reliable sources of B12 at all.

Tempeh, for example, made in the old-world, traditional manner (i.e. less hygienic) contained the bacteria that produced B12. But modern tempeh production, with its sanitary controls, have eliminated these microorganisms. Adios B12. And sea vegetables were discovered to be loaded with B12 analogues, which are sneaky, inactive forms of B12 that the body cannot use.

So what should you do? Fortunately, there are many B12 fortified foods available on the market. There are fortified breakfast cereals, meat substitutes (made from wheat gluten or soy beans), breads and pastas, and soy drinks. Be sure to always read the labels to find out B12 content.

Other popular vegan scources of B12 are fortified nutritional and brewer's yeasts. These are food yeasts (not baker's yeasts) which come as yellow flakes or in powdered form. Some brands have a pleasant, cheesy flavor, while others are bitter tasting. Again, check the labels for B12 fortification.

Is there anything else I should know about vitamin B12?

There is virtual agreement among the experts that the body is able to store B12 for many years and access it when necessary. Some believe that the body stockpiles B12 for no more than five years, while others cite evidence of a considerably longer period — up to thirty years. So if you're a vegetarian who hasn't had dairy or eggs in a few years, don't fret over B12. There's plenty of time to supplement your diet with this important nutrient.

In families with young children, pills can be a problem. An easy way to get a B12 tablet down is to crush a tablet into powder, and then add to your favorite cold drink. Mix well, serve, and repeat several times a week.

Mothers who are breastfeeding their infants should be sure to consume the RDA of B12 throughout the entire time they're nursing. While we know the body can store B12 and call up the reserves when needed, the nursing baby can't make use of this released B12. Only the B12 that a mother takes in during the breastfeeding period will find its way into the milk and to the baby.

EVENING NEWS WITH TOM BRAKALEE

"Recent studies show that vegetarians actually get more iron than meat eaters do. Which explains why anemia is less common among vegetarians."

Isn't it likely that dropping meat from the diet will lead to anemia?

That's just what the powerful meat lobby would like you to think. And it's simply not true. A number of recent studies have concluded that vegetarians actually consume more iron than do meat eaters. These conclusions add weight to the findings of other investigations which have shown that anemia — in actuality, iron-deficiency anemia — is less common among vegetarians than nonvegetarians.

Anemia is a disorder in which the blood's oxygen carriers are unable to fully carry out their normal activity. With less oxygen reaching them, and with an accompanying build-up of wastes, your cells slow down and function less effectively. While not life-threatening, the symptoms of anemia can prove quite debilitating. Most iron-deficient people experience general weakness, fatigue, dizziness, loss of appetite, and a host of other manifestations.

Several years ago, the American Dietetic Association stated that those on a meatless diet were not at a greater risk of iron deficiency than meat eaters. And what better way to "prove" all these incredible findings than to point out how few cases of iron-deficiency anemia are reported at all.

Nutrition experts advise those opting for a meatless diet that the best way to avoid iron-deficiency anemia is to eat a variety of such wholesome foods as unrefined grains, legumes, fruits, and vegetables.

Why are vegetarians less likely to become anemic?

The reason may well be that vegetarians typically devour large amounts of foods that are quite high in iron. In fact, many of these foods, like tofu, most beans, and leafy greens either equal or surpass meat as sources of iron! This must come as quite a shock to those who've been trained to view meat as the best source of iron, and a vegetarian diet as a one-way ticket to anemia. Ain't so, as the experts show.

Furthermore, some researchers conclude that vegetarians are somehow able to make much more efficient use of the iron they get from plant foods than can their counterparts who rely on meat as the source of iron. The mechanics of this special vegetarian metabolism have yet to be fully understood. But one thing's for sure: Vegetarians are getting all the iron they need — and it's coming from plant foods, not from the flesh and blood of dead animals.

Isn't it true that the iron from plant food is not well absorbed?

You bring up an excellent point. There are two types of iron found in food. Plant foods contain only one kind of iron — called non-heme iron. On the other hand, flesh foods are supplied with nearly equal portions of non-heme iron and another type, known as heme iron. Without argument, heme iron is very well absorbed. Whereas, as you suspect, non-heme iron, standing alone, is not as well assimilated.

So why don't vegetarians, en masse, develop iron-deficiency anemia? For a good reason. Mother Nature is looking out for vegetarians. As we've noted, the iron from plant foods is not well-absorbed — that is, until vitamin C is eaten along with it. Then the whole picture changes dramatically.

Suddenly, there's a spectacular increase in the availability to the body of this non-heme iron. It's no longer the poor relative. The vitamin C magically boosts plant iron to such an extent that it matches or exceeds the availability of the meat eater's heme iron.

And a vegetarian doesn't have to pop vitamin C tablets at each meal. As luck would have it, such standard vegetarian foods as fruits and vegetables are endowed with varying amounts of iron-boosting vitamin C. In fact, much of a vegetarian's diet is made up of foods high in both iron and vitamin C, making the iron in these foods easily absorbed.

Incidentally, once the body has absorbed plant iron, whether it be from lima beans or leafy greens, it's used just the same as the iron from steak.

How much iron do you need?

The recommended amounts vary based on gender. This is so, because women lose iron each month during menstruation and therefore tend towards iron deficiency. While the Recommended Dietary Allowance (RDA) for men and post-menopausal women is 10 milligrams (mg.) per day, women are advised to increase that by 50 percent, taking in 15 mg. daily. Pregnant women require even more: 30 mg. per day.

Should you pop pills to get iron? Generally, no. Nutritionists suggest that it's a better idea to get your iron from a diet of foods high in iron and vitamin C. The iron found in iron tablets isn't as easily absorbed by the body and can cause such side effects as stomach irritation, constipation, and flatulence. However, iron supplements may be necessary in special cases where a person is unable to get the RDA of iron from food sources alone. In those situations it would be best to confer with your health care provider.

MOST PLANTS ARE GOOD SOURCES OF IRON

Which vegetarian foods are particularly good sources of iron?

As you'll see, vegetarians certainly needn't miss out on iron solely because they avoid flesh foods. Dried fruits, especially prunes, raisins, figs, and apricots are extremely rich sources of iron. If you find dried fruits a bit tough to chew, simply soak them in water overnight to soften them up.

Lima beans, black-eyed peas, lentils, kidney beans, and tofu are some members of the legume family that are good places to find iron. Certain grains, such as millet, cracked wheat, quinoa, and cornmeal also contain iron in significant quantities.

Many vegetables are veritable wellsprings of iron. These include broccoli, brussels sprouts, beets, greens (like kale and mustard and dandelion greens), avocados, winter squash, mushrooms, and all the leafy green vegetables. Also, some of the sea vegetables, like arame and spirulina, are amply endowed with iron. And, of course, let's not forget Popeye's favorite: spinach. (There is some controversy over spinach, though. More about this later.) Rounding out our hit parade of iron-rich vegetarian foods would be blackstrap molasses, nutritional and brewer's yeast, and sesame seeds.

Don't forget you can dramatically increase iron absorption by eating foods that are high in vitamin C along with iron-rich foods. Some of these iron boosters include: berries, broccoli, tomatoes, citrus fruit and juices, dates, red and green peppers, cantaloupes, cabbage, brussels sprouts, and potatoes. Notice how some of these are high in both iron and vitamin C. Two for the price of one!

In order to get enough iron, don't you have to know exactly how much iron and vitamin C are in the foods you eat?

Not at all. Put aside the thought of planning your meals with a calculator and food chart. It's really not necessary to compute how much iron you're getting down to the last milligram each day.

The Recommended Dietary Allowance (RDA) is nothing more than a crude benchmark designed to cover everyone in the population. As a unique person, with your own individual nutritional needs and heredity, you may not require anything near the RDA to be healthy. Keep in mind that the RDA includes generous safety margins — excess levels of nutrients you may not need.

Also, be aware that the RDA for iron (as well as for all other essential nutrients) was conceived for meat eaters. As was noted, numerous studies suggest that vegetarians are somehow able to use the iron they absorb in a much more efficient manner than meat eaters do with their iron. The RDA doesn't even take the vegetarian's remarkable metabolism into account in determining levels of nutrients. In effect, vegetarians are playing by someone else's rules — rules which may well not apply to them.

Perhaps the best advice comes from those nutritionists who recommend that vegetarians eat heartily a wide variety of fresh fruits and vegetables, legumes, nuts and seeds, and whole grains. They point out that there's iron to be found in most everything wholesome a vegetarian eats, so without even thinking of it, you'll likely get all the iron you need.

I've heard that certain foods can interfere with iron absorption and should be avoided. What are they?

Certain chemicals found in tea and coffee, called tannins, greatly diminish iron absorption. Excessive consumption of these beverages could well result in iron deficiency. Nutritionists suggest cutting back on coffee and tea, and trying to drink them (if you must) only between meals, rather than with them, in order to reduce their iron-inhibiting effects. By the way, most herbal teas are free of tannins, making them good substitutes for regular tea.

Dairy products, too, play a role in reducing the amount of iron available to the body. Not only are milk and cheese low in iron, the calcium in these foods binds with iron and blocks its absorption. Those concerned about getting enough iron may wish to avoid dairy products altogether, or at least avoid pairing high-iron foods with high-calcium dairy foods.

Yet another iron-inhibiter, though not without some controversy, is a group of indigestible substances called phytates. These materials are found in the bran of many whole grains. Unarguably, phytates do bind with iron. However, several recent studies have shown that your digestive system seems to have the capacity to separate the phytates from the iron, and make use of the latter. On the other hand, some researchers remain skeptical and instead trust their own laboratory test tube findings, namely, that phytates inhibit iron absorption. You decide — but perhaps not until you read about fiber.

What about fiber?

It was once thought that fiber — yes, fiber — blocked iron absorption. Of course, a vegetarian diet is fiber-rich and such a pronouncement against fiber was viewed, quite naturally, with much alarm by plant food eaters. However, recent studies have shown that this issue is not as clear cut as once believed. Results from a recent, monumental study in China paradoxically demonstrated that a diet rich in fiber, as well as in phytates, did nothing to diminish the availability of iron to the body.

Let's debunk another myth. This one about spinach. Earlier opinions had it that the iron in spinach was in the form of iron oxalates — a particularly difficult substance to absorb. As a result, many vegetarians shunned iron-rich spinach. But, as a consequence of newer research, many experts now suggest that the intake of moderate amounts of these oxalates will not interfere with iron absorption.

Regardless of the findings which may come from future investigations of iron inhibitors, vegetarians are advised to continue eating the iron-rich foods commonly found in the plant food kingdom. And, in addition to consuming foods high in vitamin C to boost iron absorption, vegetarians can do one more thing to enhance their iron intake.

What's that?

Literally, eat iron. However, I'm not talking about ingots at every meal. But by using iron skillets and pots, vegetarians can add some pretty hefty amounts of iron to their diet. Studies indicate that the iron content of foods can be increased up to four times when prepared in iron cookware. This is quite an iron-boosting feat!

Still, for this process to work, there are a few things you should be aware of. Iron will indeed leave the pot or skillet and enter the food, but only when that food is acidic and being cooked for a while. Tomato sauce is ideally suited for helping liberate iron from your iron cookware. And slow-cooking provides the necessary time for the mineral to migrate into the cooked food. A quick stir fry in oil or butter will not do the trick.

How do vegetarians manage to get enough calcium?

Have you seen many (or any?) vegetarians whose teeth have fallen out or who suffer from weak bones and hip fractures? Probably not. Yet many newcomers to vegetarianism (and especially their parents!) worry that they might not be picking up sufficient calcium. Not to worry.

Vegetarians who include milk, cheese, and yogurt in their diets usually have no problems meeting the Recommended Dietary Allowance for calcium. On the other hand, vegans (vegetarians who avoid dairy and eggs) would appear to be good candidates for calcium deficiency. And without drinking milk, how could they possibly get enough calcium?

Actually, many plant foods are richly endowed with calcium. Excellent sources include such greens as broccoli, spinach, collards, and kale. Soybeans, tempeh, sesame seeds, fortified soy drinks, vegetables, figs, sea vegetables, molasses, and almonds are some other places you can find appreciable amounts of calcium. Also, tofu can be a major source of calcium — but you'll have to check the package label. Tofu that's been made using calcium sulfate (also called gypsum) as the thickening agent will be significantly higher in calcium than tofu made with other solidifiers.

So, how's all this plant food stack up against the "king" of calcium — milk? You might be surprised. The same amount of calcium that's found in one cup of milk (nearly one-third of your daily requirement) can also be found in two tablespoons of blackstrap molasses, or in one cup of cooked greens, or in four ounces of tofu. And these are just a few comparisons.

As we've seen, milk products don't have a monopoly on calcium. In fact, and this probably goes against everything you've ever heard or seen in the milk ads, the calcium obtained from plant sources may be better utilized by your body than the calcium found in cow's milk.

But how could that possibly be?

Mother Nature designed cow's milk specifically for baby calves, not for baby people. And long before cows were invented (or at least domesticated), and for some time prior to the creation of the American dairy industry, human beings were slowly evolving and growing strong, healthy bones by ingesting all the calcium they needed from plant food sources. (Besides, no other animal on earth drinks milk beyond a short infancy — let alone the milk of another species!)

Studies have shown that a diet high in animal protein and saturated fat not only blocks the absorption of calcium, but also causes the body to excrete calcium through the kidneys into the urine. What's this got to do with milk? Milk is high in both protein and saturated fat. As such, milk is its own worst enemy when it comes to being a provider of calcium. In fact, the excessive protein and saturated fat in milk cause your body's calcium reserves to actually fall.

How does that happen?

Saturated fat, such as that found in milk, latches on to calcium and creates a mixture that the body has difficulty in absorbing. However, aside from being a calcium-blocker, milk is a high, animal-protein food. And numerous studies have shown that an excess of animal proteins in the diet leads to a sharp increase in blood acid levels. In order to get back into critical balance, the body neutralizes the highly acidic blood by pouring in calcium that's been taken from bone. Incidentally, research strongly suggests that plant proteins do not have this same deleterious effect on the body.

It's a cruel irony, that by drinking milk and eating cheese for the purpose of obtaining calcium, you're actually losing it. And the more dairy products you consume, the greater your loss of calcium. Even if you flood your body with calcium, a high-protein diet (such as the standard American diet!) leaches calcium from your bones faster than you can absorb it.

But aren't there substances in many plant foods that block calcium absorption?

That's just what the dairy lobby would like you to think. For years, some researchers have argued that plant foods are loaded with oxalates, phytates, and fiber that prevent calcium from being absorbed. But these adverse claims have not been based on real-world situations, only on lab experiments and test tube results. The human body is a bit more complex than that.

A number of nutritionists are of the opinion that while these "blocking" agents may well be present in some plant foods, the human digestive system is somehow able to overcome their potentially injurious effects. And long-term, epidemiological studies bear that out. Vegetarians do not suffer from any calcium deficiency diseases. In fact, bone density (a measure of bone strength) in vegetarians is as great or greater than that of their meat eating counterparts. Furthermore, on account of their low-protein, low-fat diet, aging vegetarians lose bone-mass much slower, and suffer far less from osteoporosis than do meat eaters.

In practice, most sensible vegetarians rely on a variety of whole foods to supply their calcium needs. Thus, if any particular food were deficient in calcium, or contained a so-called "blocker," then the other foods would easily compensate. And some vegetarians even choose to err on the safe side by supplementing their diet with calcium pills — made from non-animal sources, of course.

I'm confused. We're continually advised to get lots of calcium to avoid osteoporosis. How can that be wrong?

You have a right to feel perplexed, even angry, at discovering that such traditional guidance has been absolutely worthless at preventing such a serious disease as osteoporosis.

After all, over 50 years ago, researchers reported their findings that diets high in animal protein (dairy products included) caused the body to excrete significant quantities of calcium. And studies around the world have pointed out that the highest rates of osteoporosis are found in those nations which consume the most dairy products.

What is osteoporosis? It's a crippling disease caused by the severe loss of calcium from the bones, which leaves them porous and brittle. These weakened bones then easily split and crack. Major breaks, such as fractures of the hip, are both common and a leading cause of death in the elderly. Osteoporosis casts a wide net. It affects millions of Americans: one in ten is afflicted, while nearly 50,000 die from it each year.

Yet the public has been led to believe that only by consuming large amounts of calcium, especially from dairy products, can osteoporosis be prevented. The dairy industry, long owning a cash cow in milk, has led the way in so "educating" the public; it also has financed much research at major universities to "prove" that every body needs milk to ward off bone disease.

But that couldn't be further from the truth. Numerous studies have revealed that it's the excessive animal-protein in the diet that causes the bones to shed calcium in great amounts, leading to osteoporosis. Unfortunately, the meat and dairy industries have managed to shift the focus away from that finding in order to continue to sell their products.

And the public (including many nutritionists who should know better) believes that osteoporosis is an inevitable condition of aging, which only can be averted by consuming large quantities of calcium — especially that obtained from cow's milk. But it's really futile. Until the consumption of animal protein is drastically reduced, your body will continue to lose more calcium than it could ever take in. And osteoporosis will continue as an epidemic. The issue here is animal-protein excess, not calcium deficiency.

Many researchers believe that it's because of their lower protein consumption that vegetarians lose little bone as they mature. And studies bear this out. Measurements of bone mass show that aging vegetarians retain twice the calcium levels in their bones as do their meat-eating, milk-drinking counterparts. Furthermore, studies here and abroad conclude that vegetarians are definitely at a reduced risk of ever developing osteoporosis.

Aren't those scare stories about all the chemicals found in meat really overdoing it a bit?

Unfortunately, they're not exaggerating at all. Producing beef is no mom and pop operation. With annual sales in the tens of billions of dollars, meat producers employ every trick in the book to maximize profits — including the widespread use of hundreds of drugs. In fact, beef producers administer more drugs to cattle than physicians prescribe for their patients. The pharmaceutical industry would suffer a major depression if their chief customers — the cattlemen — were required to raise animals without chemicals.

Why are those drugs necessary? Because cattle spend the last few months of their lives in unwholesome, disease-ridden feedlots being fattened up for slaughter. And an environment in which cattle are shoulder to shoulder, often knee-deep in their own manure, is not conducive to good health. To keep a multitude of cattle diseases under control, cattlemen regularly furnish various antibiotics to the animals. Incredibly, powerful residues of such antibiotics as penicillin and tetracycline show up in steaks, burgers, and other meat products and cannot be cooked out. These chemicals enter the human body and wreak havoc on human bacteria so vital for good health.

Cattle feed alone contains an abundance of frightening chemicals. Pesticide-treated grains and slaughterhouse byproducts (themselves loaded with drug residues) are common livestock food. And potent chemicals, not approved for human consumption, are legally permitted to be used for treating this fodder. These ingested toxins, by the way, are not magically flushed out of the animals — instead, they become more and more concentrated in the flesh.

And then there are the growth hormones. These drugs are dispensed to cattle to accelerate their development. It saves feedlot owners millions of dollars worth of grains to be able to fatten up the livestock quickly and artificially (that is, with less feed than normally required). Even after the animals are slaughtered, these hormones remain in the meat. Then, after being eaten, these intense stimulants accumulate in humans. And the evidence is strong that these hormones initiate and encourage the development of various cancers.

There's more.

• Animals are drugged with tranquilizers to reduce the stress caused by extremely congested living quarters.

• Since modern livestock production denies any exercise to the animals (because developing their muscles would make the meat tough), metabolic wastes build up and are sealed in the animal carcass after slaughter.

• Dangerous, drug-resistant bacteria survive the animal's demise and can appear in meat purchased by the consumer.

• Just before slaughter, the terror-stricken cattle release considerable amounts of adrenalin into the body. This "natural" hormone remains in the animal flesh long after the butcher has finished carving.

It's stunning to think of the long-term health consequences of consuming meat — clearly an unwholesome product containing powerful residues of antibiotics, hormones, pesticides, tranquilizers, microorganisms, and toxic waste products.

What's really in hot dogs?

Are you sure you want to know? Frankfurters, as well as most other processed meats, like sausages, bologna, and salami, can legally be made up of a hefty amount of indelicate animal remains. When run through colossal meat grinders, such remnants as connective tissue, cartilage, bone marrow, and pulverized bone lose their individuality and become known as "mechanically separated meat." That's the stuff in every hot dog you wolf down.

Other unseemly ingredients have been known to find their way into processed meats. Now and again, a diseased or cancerous animal carcass will have a tumor, a blood clot, or even an entire section cut out and the rest sold as meat. As past scandals have revealed, unscrupulous processors have incorporated these tumors, clots, and cancerous organs into meat mixes for the manufacture of hot dogs.

On top of all this, carcass flesh remnants are loaded with fat and cholesterol; and bone remnants contain measurable concentrations of radioactive elements and toxic heavy metals.

And last but not least, are the great numbers of disease-producing bacteria found in processed meats. Every step of the way, from slaughter to meat department display case, the ever-decaying meat is contaminated by workers and equipment that are not models of meticulous hygiene.

Add to this the negligence of processors who store the putrefying meat at improper temperatures and undercook it. Under these conditions, bacteria propagate to such extremes that they practically jump out at you in each bite of hot dog.

The upshot of all this is mild food poisoning for millions of Americans. But they're the "lucky" ones. Because for a very small number of youngsters and senior citizens whose immune systems are too weak to ward off such vast quantities of microorganisms — eating hot dogs can literally bring on sudden death.

Isn't chicken more healthful than red meat?

Hardly. Much like cattle raised on overcrowded feedlots, chickens (and turkeys, too) are raised in factory-like settings. The birds spend their whole lives tightly packed in tiny cages that fill huge cavernous rooms in which the lights shine brightly 24 hours a day. A more unnatural existence would be hard to imagine.

These abysmal conditions cause a wide variety of

poultry diseases, as well as so much stress that the birds would peck each other to death if not for outside intervention. Enter the poultrymen who administer antibiotics to ward off sicknesses (and promote weight gain) and tranquilizers to calm the chickens (and lessen their interest in killing one another). The birds are also sprayed with toxic chemicals to kill such vermin as ticks and lice.

As with beef, chicken purchased by consumers contains potent residues of all the dreadful antibiotics, stimulants, depressants, and pesticides routinely added to chicken feed — itself a hodgepodge of various chemicals, drugs, and slaughterhouse waste products. On top of it all, add another indelicate fact. Chickens, under the usual, appalling factory conditions, typically eat each other's feces.

Are you as likely to get food poisoning from chicken as from red meat?

A consequence of the poultry industry's routine use of pharmaceuticals is the emergence of virulent strains of microbes that are increasingly resistant to antibiotics. When you eat chicken, you harbor microorganisms that have the potential of causing serious intestinal infections, against which the usual life-saving drugs have less and less potency. It's especially hazardous for young and old people alike, as their immune systems are not at full strength.

Chicken is typically tainted by bacteria in many ways. Modern poultry slaughterhouses employ automated equipment to process the birds. While the machinery is fast —

some 5,000 birds are eviscerated each hour at a typical facility — it's often sloppy. And during this process, it's not uncommon for birds to be accidentally ripped apart, spraying guts and feces everywhere. Bacteria go wild.

Prior to evisceration, contamination can also occur while the birds are being mechanically defeathered. As mechanical fingers pound the chickens, feces is unintentionally pressed out of the birds, smearing them with a microbe-rich goop. During this operation, bacteria are forced deep into the bird's skin pores, where they survive chemical sprays and other attempts to kill them.

From what occurs in the slaughterhouse alone (not to mention the unsanitary conditions that poultry encounters en route to the grocery store), the chicken you purchase stands a good chance of being a carrier of salmonella and other disease-causing microbes.

It's hardly surprising that almost 75 percent of poultry inspectors interviewed by the *Atlanta Journal-Constitution* several years ago, based on what they observed in the slaughterhouses, decided to quit eating chicken.

I DON'T WANT THE KIDS OUT PLAYING IN THIS TOO LONG. THE WATER'S FULL OF INDUSTRIAL WASTES, TOXINS, PESTICIDE RUNOFF, AND HEAVY METALS.

Since fish grow up in their own natural habitat, aren't they a wholesome substitute for all other meats?

You be the judge after hearing the startling facts. Those who eat seafood for health reasons should realize that before arriving on the dinner plates, their fish spent their entire lives in some pretty murky waters. Rivers, streams, lakes, coastal waters, oceans — everywhere you find fish — are veritable chemical soups of such pollutants as industrial toxins (like PCB's), toxic metals, and pesticides (runoff from farms and feedlots).

Now imagine dropping a sponge into a vat of water that's been contaminated by these chemicals and poisons. The sponge would soon be saturated with deadly substances. That's just what happens to fish because they absorb toxic chemicals from the water passing over their gills. They literally breathe in the poisonous gunk and store it in their fatty tissues. What's more, fish can accumulate incredible concentrations of toxins — often, millions of times the potency of the chemicals found in their watery habitat.

There are other serious problems with fish. Most of the seafoods found in retail display cases are caught on the high seas by huge fishing ships. After being hauled out of the water, the fish are shovelled into storage holds. As fish pile up upon fish, the great weight presses their guts, spilling their microbe-rich intestinal contents on each other. In an attempt to counter these teeming bacteria, fishing crews spray their catches with powerful antibiotic solutions.

By the time the fish have reached land, they've been contaminated by chemicals and microorganisms, and have suffered damage from being hauled aboard ship and dumped below deck. Already in a state of spoilage, the fish are eviscerated, boned, and sliced — processes which spread the surface bacteria and toxins deep into the fish flesh. Further bacterial growth and contamination occur as the processed fish make their way to the wholesaler and then to the retailer.

What's the bottom line? Fish contaminants have been linked to human cancers as well as to other alarming health problems, like hepatitis, kidney and liver failure, birth defects, and acute food poisoning. For many whose remaining flesh food is fish — it's enough to go quickly and completely vegetarian.

Despite knowing the dangers of eating flesh foods, I can't imagine any society going vegetarian, can you?

What's so hard to visualize? Several times in this century that scenario was actually played out, as entire populations became vegetarians — and suffered intolerably good health as a result. I'll concede, however, that national emergencies were really behind it all.

During the first world war, the British fleet blockaded the North Sea in order to deny Germany its vital imports. Most affected by this action was Denmark — whose three million people were abruptly cut off from their normal, lavish pre-war supplies of meat. In order to ward off starvation, the Danish government turned to the head of the Danish vegetarian society for guidance.

The government was advised to stop feeding the nation's grains and other plant food to livestock. And do what with it? Feed people, of course! Thus began a unique effort in which an entire country fed itself a vegetarian diet consisting mostly of whole grains, potatoes, green vegetables, fruits, and limited dairy products. Despite the hardships of economic warfare, there was more than enough food for all Danes. And then, after one year, something extraordinary was noticed. The death rate from all causes dropped a startling 34 percent below the level of the previous two decades. No other nation up to that time had ever had a lower mortality rate!

Not only had no one starved, but also the health of the nation had improved strikingly on a vegetarian diet. All might have gone on happily ever after, but with the end of the war the Danes were no longer deprived of their meat. As flesh food consumption resumed its high level, death rates and incidents of heart and circulatory diseases skyrocketed to their unhealthy pre-war levels.

Several decades later, another war emergency made

temporary vegetarians of the Swiss and Norwegians. They too discovered, albeit fleetingly, how the health of a whole nation can improve spectacularly by following a meatless diet.

Besides the hormone and antibiotic residues found in meat, shouldn't you be worrying about all the fat, too?

You're absolutely right! Considerable evidence links the consumption of saturated fat and cholesterol (both found chiefly in flesh foods) with heart attacks, strokes, and several types of cancer.

Meat eaters who have a yen for such flesh foods as ribs, cold cuts, burgers, hot dogs, bacon, or even sirloin, should consider this: These meats are crammed with fat. More than 75 percent of the calories from each of those meats are calories from fat. Incredible, but true.

When you stop to realize that Americans are among the heaviest meat eaters on the planet, it shouldn't be all that surprising that one of every two people you know will either die of heart disease; colon, prostate, or breast cancer; or of other causes directly attributable to high-fat diets.

Furthermore, autopsies done on young people killed in accidents reveal hardened arteries, fat deposits, and scar tissue — classic manifestations of heart disease. These are teenagers, not mature adults or seniors. Appallingly, even children not yet of the age to be in kindergarten have been found to be in the early stages of heart and coronary artery disease. All this as a result of following the standard American diet that's rich in fat and cholesterol.

Isn't it true that we'd be a lot closer to preventing heart disease simply by eating chicken and fish instead of red meat?

No. There's not much of a difference whether you eat beef, bird, or bass. The edible portions of these animals are primarily made up of muscle. And muscle, in spite of its healthy connotations, is a storehouse of fat and cholesterol.

Studies have demonstrated that those who eschew red meat in favor of chicken or fish do not have appreciably lower blood cholesterol levels than those of red meat eaters. In other words, the body's response to chicken or fish is the same as that for beef: blood cholesterol rises to unhealthy levels.

Understandably, this myth that poultry and seafood are healthier is widely believed, even among many nutritionists, because there's actually a partial — but flawed — truth to it. Let me explain. Admittedly, chicken and fish are lower in saturated fat than red meat. And as you know, the less saturated fat the better. So far so good!

But here's the rub. Calorie for calorie, chicken and fish contain nearly twice the cholesterol that beef has. We're talking about major cholesterol here. So while they're low in one deadly fat (saturated fat), chicken and fish are very high in another (cholesterol). Which is worse for you: chicken, fish, or beef? It pretty much looks like a dead heat.

I'm always hearing about saturated, monounsaturated, polyunsaturated, and hydrogenated fats. What do they mean?

Get ready for a quick trip through the land of Grease. Fats are divided generally into three categories — saturated, monounsaturated, and polyunsaturated. Let's begin by profiling the "bad" fat.

Saturated fat is found in animal foods like meat, eggs, and dairy products. Any fat that's firm at room temperature is a saturated one. You've seen these solid fats as the marbled streaks in meat, as butter, as cheese, and as fat globs in chicken and fish. Why does saturated fat get such bad press? Because it has a nasty tendency to raise blood cholesterol levels. This leads to the accumulation of cholesterol on artery walls. And before you know it, an artery is completely plugged up; then a stroke or heart attack can result from the interruption of blood normally carried by the blocked artery.

Another saturated fat, though not of animal origin, is hydrogenated fat. This is nothing more than regular, liquid vegetable oil that's undergone a complete chemical makeover (called "hydrogenation") to become solid. It's best to avoid hydrogenated fat as it has the same injurious effect on the body as does saturated animal fat.

On the other hand, polyunsaturated and monounsaturated fats supply substances called essential fatty acids which are needed for a healthy cardiovascular system. Studies suggest that replacing saturated fat with "poly" and "mono" fats could help lower blood cholesterol levels and greatly reduce the risks of developing heart disease. These good-hearted fats are found in the staples of a vegetarian diet: whole grains, beans, peas, lentils, nuts and seeds, and in such oils as safflower, corn, canola, peanut, soy, and olive.

IF YOU WANT LOW-FAT, YOU'LL HAVE TO GO NEXT DOOR TO THE VEGETARIAN DELI.

STEW MEAT

SPECIAL RIBS

SAVE

How much fat do we need, anyway?

A lot less than you think. Various national health organizations, including the American Dietetic Association, suggest that you limit your daily fat intake to 30 percent of your calories. Although many researchers believe that figure is much too high, most Americans ignore all recommendations and wolf down nearly 50 percent of their calories from fat. That's a diet of one-half fat!

Few peoples on earth eat as much grease as do Americans. And the appalling statistics of deaths from heart disease and cancer must surely be viewed as evidence that something's terribly wrong with the national diet.

A considerable number of nutritionists agree that while young children require a diet that's 30 percent fat, adults certainly do not. They recommend that adults cut back their daily fat consumption to about 10-15 percent of calories in order to decrease their risks of developing life-threatening disorders.

Isn't there an easy way for you to keep track of your fat intake without worrying about percentages, calculators, and food charts?

You bet there is! Forget all about the algebraic gymnastics needed to compute the fat percentage of each morsel you press between your lips. Eating is a celebration, not rockpile duty!

The simplest, most natural way to insure that you're getting only the small amount of fat your body needs, is to follow a vegetarian diet made up basically of unrefined grains, wholewheat breads and pastas, legumes (beans, peas, and lentils), fruits, and vegetables. These are nature's own low-fat foods. How low? Less than 20 percent fat. And the less fat you eat, the better your odds of living a long life; especially one that's free of the coronary diseases and cancers that ravage eaters of high-fat flesh foods.

Can a healthful vegetarian diet include fatty foods like butter, cheese, eggs, and avocados?

You raise a good point. Even vegetarians can put themselves at risk for heart disease and cancer by following a diet high in fat. And whether that fat comes from plants or from animals, fat is still fat.

A wholesome vegetarian diet may include, but only in modest quantities, such rich foods as nuts, seeds, eggs, olives, margarine, peanut butter, coconuts, avocados, cheese, ice cream, mayonnaise, and tofu. (It may be hard to believe, but tofu, all by itself, is 50 percent fat!) When consumed only as condiments, however, these high-fat foods won't pose any serious risks.

This is as good a time as any to take another look at those "good" fats — polyunsaturates and monounsaturates. While they may indeed have healthful properties, they too must be limited in the diet. Why? Because all oils, even those from organically grown sources, are 100 percent fat! And too much of any fat can make even the strictest vegetarian obese and sickly.

A vegetarian diet, comprised of a variety of whole grains, legumes, fruits, and vegetables, is naturally low-fat and provides all that the body requires. But yes, a little cheating is okay. Getting just a little extra fat from non-hydrogenated vegetable oils, and from those foods mentioned above will probably wreak no havoc on your body.

Since there's a strong connection between heart disease and cholesterol, shouldn't you try to completely eliminate cholesterol from your body?

If you were somehow able to do just that, you'd be knocking at heaven's gate awfully soon. Why? Because cholesterol is actually so important to your well being (it's involved in fat digestion, and hormone and vitamin production) that your body manufactures all that it needs.

However, cholesterol is a good thing — up to a point. When there's more of the stuff than you need swimming in the blood it can cause arterial damage and plugged arteries. Eventually, the blood won't be able to get beyond these obstructions and the result can be a stroke or heart attack.

Okay. So what causes this rise in blood cholesterol levels? When you eat red meats, chicken, and fish, as well as their byproducts, like eggs, milk, butter and cheese, you dump a lot of cholesterol into your blood. And though the body is being swamped with cholesterol, it still continues with the critical task of making this substance. The result, of course, is a cholesterol overdose; which, as we've noted, leads to cardiovascular disease.

Incidentally, animal foods are the only source of cholesterol. Plant foods contain none at all. That's right. Grains, beans, fruits, vegetables, nuts, and seeds don't have a speck of cholesterol.

Besides ingesting cholesterol-rich animal foods, there's another way (which even most vegetarians aren't aware of) for blood cholesterol levels to get jacked up.

What way is that?

Eating foods that are high in saturated fats, just like eating cholesterol-rich foods, will elevate blood cholesterol levels. The more saturated fat in the diet, the higher the cholesterol levels will climb. While the exact mechanisms involved aren't fully understood, saturated fats somehow stimulate the liver to increase its output of cholesterol.

Interestingly enough, certain vegetable fats (namely, coconut and palm oils, and cocoa butter) are also saturated fats. And though they contain no cholesterol (remember, there's not a drop of cholesterol in any plant foods), these vegetable fats, being saturated ones, will raise blood cholesterol just as surely as will any saturated animal fat.

Also, hydrogenated oils and products made from these "saturated" oils (like margarine and shortening) will raise the cholesterol level. It's certainly not impossible even for the strict vegetarian who eats no saturated animal fats to have elevated cholesterol. This unhealthy situation could be brought about by overloading the diet with such saturated vegetable fats as avocados, chocolates, nuts, margarine, hydrogenated oils, palm and coconut oils, nut butters, olives, and coconut.

In fact, some researchers suggest that consuming too much of any fat, whether it be animal or vegetable, saturated or unsaturated (even including the wholesome polyunsaturated and monounsaturated fats), causes the liver to produce more cholesterol than the body needs.

Just how does a fatty diet lead to hardening of the arteries, anyway?

The condition you refer to goes by another name, one harder to pronounce and remember: atherosclerosis. This medical term more accurately describes what takes place within the arteries of long-term flesh food eaters. **Athero** refers to a tumor or lump; **sclerosis** means the abnormal hardening of cells and tissues. Even within the arteries of young meat eaters, minute lumps form on the inside surfaces of arterial walls.

Let's see how all this gets started. Recall, that all red meats, poultry, and seafood are high in saturated fat and cholesterol. Eating these flesh foods not only dumps large amounts of fat into your blood vessels, it also makes your blood cholesterol levels soar. As a result of this fat overload, any number of points in the linings of the arteries will develop deposits of fatty substances.

Over the years, if the diet continues with flesh foods, these fatty accumulations will grow larger and more solid, reducing blood flow through the affected arteries. Ultimately, the arteries become completely blocked and blood flow is halted.

If the blocked artery happens to be a major one supplying blood to the heart, a heart attack will occur. If one of the brain's major suppliers of blood is blocked, the result will be a stroke. Of course, a blocked artery may simply come under so much pressure that it bursts. Such a catastrophic explosion in the brain, for example, could result in sudden death or permanent paralysis.

America's love affair with greasy, high-fat foods can be blamed for yet another ailment besides heart attacks and strokes. And while not life-threatening, it's a condition millions of men have trouble talking about.

What is it?

Impotence. A disorder in which the male is unable to attain an erection during sexual activity. And it's not something that afflicts merely a few souls in their nineties. In fact, many younger men make up the 10 to 15 million Americans who simply can't "get it up."

Long thought to be chiefly caused by psychological problems, impotence is now recognized, along with cardiovascular disease, as yet another likely consequence of the average American's fondness for high-fat and high-cholesterol foods.

Recall that a heart attack or stroke results when a major artery carrying blood to the heart or brain becomes blocked by a cholesterol plug — a condition referred to as atherosclerosis. And without their vital supplies of blood, those organs suffer severe damage, usually leading to sudden death.

Well, just as the brain and heart need blood to carry out their duties, so too does the penis need blood to perform its vital function of propagation, specifically, of getting an erection at the proper time. However, atherosclerosis can cause major problems by blocking the large blood vessels which normally supply the penis with that extra surge of blood needed to give it an erection. And without that additional blood supply, the penis won't be rising for any occasion.

Can your crystal ball predict when there might be a cure for atherosclerosis?

There's no need to crystal gaze at all. The evidence is already in. And it's all good news — especially since most Americans have already developed atherosclerosis. That's right. Anyone raised on the standard American diet of foods rich in fat and cholesterol is today walking around with "hardening of the arteries." For many people, the disease has already progressed to ominous stages.

Not long ago, it was assumed that once your arteries got gummed up with fatty deposits (or more precisely: plaque-clogged) there was little for you to do but wait for the grim reaper. However, recent studies have completely discredited that foolish notion.

Due in part to the research of Dean Ornish, M.D., and John McDougall, M.D., it's now known that a low-fat vegetarian diet can actually help the body clean out plaque-clogged arteries; in effect, reversing the advance of heart disease. Certainly that's nothing less than life-saving news for those with advanced atherosclerosis. It just goes to show that you're never too old to turn over a new leafy green.

Why are meat eaters more likely than vegetarians to develop cancer?

Of the many factors that play a role in causing breast cancer in women, and prostate cancer in men, a high-fat diet now appears to be the most culpable. Many researchers believe that women whose diets are rich in flesh foods, dairy products, and eggs, have elevated levels of female sex hormones, called estrogens, in the blood. This is a particularly dangerous situation since estrogens are thought to promote abnormal breast tissue activity linked to cancer.

Around the world, studies uniformly show that nations with the greatest fat consumption suffer the highest rates of breast cancer. Conversely, where fat intake is low, breast cancer is a negligible health risk. Not so in the U.S., where over 50,000 women die from breast cancer each year (as great a figure as all the American troops killed in the entire war in Vietnam).

On the other hand, studies of vegetarian women revealed that, as a group, they were at reduced risk of breast cancer due to their low estrogen blood levels. The diet they followed contained relatively little fat and was richly endowed with fiber and complex carbohydrates. Of course, the standard American diet is completely contrary to a vegetarian diet, hence the appalling frequency of breast cancer in the general population.

At the same time, a diet high in animal fats, will likewise cause a man's blood hormone levels to soar. These powerful substances floating in the blood stimulate the growth of certain tissues in the prostate. This organ responds by dramatically expanding in size. And the likelihood of prostate cancer is greatly increased.

But that's not all. Meat eating has been linked to yet another deadly cancer.

Which one?

Colon cancer. One of the lesser publicized cancers that quietly, but efficiently, sends nearly 70,000 Americans to an early grave each year.

Recently, many studies have been published that clearly incriminate meat consumption as a major cause of colon cancer. Again, a look around the world shows that societies that eat little meat experience this deadly disease far less frequently than do typical meat-eating Americans.

Researchers have found that high-fat and high-cholesterol intakes (from eating flesh foods) stimulate the body into manufacturing abnormally large quantities of digestive aids, called bile acids. This is a dangerous development since an excess of these acids has been shown to promote the formation of tumors in the colon. And recall, if you will, that large amounts of fat (unavoidable when you eat meat) have a hormone-like effect of stimulating the growth of existing tumors and other pre-cancerous lumps.

However, on a vegetarian diet your body produces only scant amounts of bile acids. This is because plant foods don't require much in the way of caustic substances in order to break down and be assimilated, as do flesh foods.

Furthermore, the role of fiber (or lack of it) as a causative factor in colon cancer cannot be overlooked. All flesh foods — whether it be beef, pork, poultry, or seafood — provide no fiber whatsoever. This accounts for the long time that waste products sit in the meat eater's colon awaiting stool formation and a bowel movement.

And the longer these toxic wastes remain in the colon, the greater the likelihood of injury and mutation occuring within the cells that line the bowel wall. This is not a likely scenario for vegetarians since their waste products are exceptionally high in fiber (and missing the stimulants, hormones, antibiotics, excessive pesticides, and high fat and cholesterol found in all flesh foods) which allows for quick stool formation and easy elimination. This speedy transit time and lack of exposure to meat-derived carcinogens are perhaps the chief reasons why vegetarians suffer much less colon cancer than meat eaters do.

I usually feel sleepy after eating meat. Why's that?

The reason for it can be stated in just one word: FAT! Becoming drowsy after finishing a high-fat, meat dish is yet another side effect of eating flesh foods.

How does that happen? Well, let's take a quick look at your circulatory system to understand this phenomenon. Within your blood vessels, countless blood cells carry nutrients and oxygen to various organs. These cells are champion swimmers — bobbing and weaving around all the other cells similarly making the rounds. When they do collide, they simply recoil, and then continue on their way.

However, soon after you eat meat, your bloodstream gets flooded with fat from the food. Quickly, the blood cells become coated with fat, and are unable to function as the artful dodgers they recently were. Instead of bouncing off one another upon impact, they stick together and form globs. In short order, the blood vessels are crammed with these greasy clumps and blood flow is slowed to a crawl. In fact, some of the smaller blood vessels are so congested that no blood reaches them at all.

What all this means is that your tissues and organs have been temporarily deprived of their regular quotas of nutrients and oxygen. And with less oxygen reaching your brain, it should come as no surprise that you feel like dozing off. Fortunately, just a few hours later, like ice melting in the warm afternoon sun, the fatty clumps break up. Blood again flows to all the organs, and your head clears.

If you're like the typical American, though, you'll have another high-fat, flesh food meal in a couple of hours and the whole process will begin anew. Oh, you might even try to fight off the fatigue with a stimulating beverage that's high in caffeine, like coffee or a cola. And while this jolt may temporarily do the trick, consuming too much caffeine is not good for your health.

Is it really any wonder that many meat eaters drag from pillar to post constantly tuckered out?

Two vegetarians I know are always eating — I mean always — yet manage to keep slim. Why aren't they fat?

Wouldn't it be refreshing to have one less affliction to worry about? Well, obesity is just such a disorder that most vegetarians don't lose any sleep over. That's because a vegetarian regimen of grains, legumes, fruits, and vegetables is naturally low in calories (while all flesh foods are just the opposite). And by abstaining from high-calorie flesh foods, vegetarians can scarf down mounds of foodstuffs without gaining any weight. In fact, obese people in transition to vegetarianism discover that they're able to fill up to their heart's (and stomach's) content on low-fat vegetarian foods — and lose weight effortlessly. This is quite an "austere" diet: You eat more food than you've ever eaten in your life and get a trim figure in the process.

What with all the overweight Americans searching for the easy (and healthy!) way to shed unwanted fat, it's really quite astonishing that they've not yet discovered this magical side effect of a vegetarian diet. Of course, another side effect is that vegetarians are at reduced risk of developing such maladies as cardiovascular disease, cancer, high blood pressure, osteoporosis, and diabetes.

And recently, researchers have unearthed some provocative data which may help further explain why vegetarians are such a lean bunch.

What were those findings?

In essence, researchers discovered that you get fat not merely be eating too many calories, but by consuming too many **fat** calories. In other words, eating fat makes you fat; eating carbohydrates does not. A vegetarian diet is rich in complex carbohydrate calories (from whole grains, legumes, fruits, and vegetables) while a flesh foods diet is chock-full of saturated fat calories.

In reviewing the data from nearly a century of dietary studies, researchers noticed something curious. Namely, that while contemporary Americans are consuming less calories than their recent ancestors, the average weight of a typical American is higher than ever before. What's the meaning of this? Read on.

Also, several contemporary studies showed that the plumpest persons were those who ate the least total calories, while those who ate the most calories generally had the leanest frames. Had the world turned upside down? But, by examining what each individual ate, it was observed that those who ate the most total calories ate far fewer fat calories than the chubby participants. This has a direct bearing on why vegetarians are leaner than their meat eating counterparts. Because a vegetarian diet is naturally low in fat, vegetarians are consuming far fewer fat calories than are meat eaters. Remember, eating fat makes you fat.

And while these findings don't really give vegetarians license to go hog wild over their naturally high carbohydrate diet, it does let them fill up on whichever wholesome foods they desire without having to worry about counting each and every calorie. And why mar such a joyous occasion as eating, by fretting over calories?

Would a vegetarian diet benefit a diabetic?

For most diabetics it's nothing short of miraculous how a simple change to a vegetarian diet reduces their suffering and helps prevent such "inevitable" long-term complications as blindness, hardening of the arteries, and kidney failure. Numerous studies have confirmed that a vegetarian diet — one that's naturally low in fat, high in fiber, and rich in unrefined foods — gives the vast majority of diabetics enough control to reduce or even eliminate their insulin medication.

What exactly is diabetes?

Diabetes is actually two distinct diseases. Type I (also called insulin-dependent or juvenile onset diabetes) comes about because the pancreas fails to produce enough insulin to meet the body's needs. Typically, victims of this type of diabetes are young people not yet out of their teens.

On the other hand, the Type II (known as non-insulin dependent or adult onset diabetes) sufferer produces plenty of insulin. But this insulin is somehow impaired, and the body is unable to utilize it. Type II diabetics represent the vast majority (up to 90 percent) of diabetes victims.

All diabetics, regardless of type, share an inability to properly digest their food. Let's look at a non-diabetic for a moment. In a normal, healthy person, a great deal of the food that's eaten is turned into glucose, or blood sugar.

This glucose is the fuel that each cell of each organ requires to carry on their life-sustaining functions.

But to be utilized, blood sugar must get into each cell. It can't just jump in from the bloodstream. Something has got to transfer the blood sugar from the blood into the cells. This is where insulin enters the picture. In a healthy person, the pancreas secretes just the right amount of useful insulin required to "carry" the glucose into each cell. Thus, with the help of a carrier (insulin), the cells are able to convert the blood sugar into life-giving energy.

But this is not the scenario in a diabetic, whose blood sugar remains in the blood outside each cell, unable to get in because of either the lack of insulin (Type I) or the presence of non-functional insulin (Type II).

What happens next?

Without blood sugar to consume, the cells of a diabetic will face starvation and even death. Of course, if the cells die, so does the body. Thus, to deal with such a crisis, the body will quickly begin burning something else for the vital energy it needs to carry on. That "something else" is fat. But that's only a temporary fix because the rapid burning of large amounts of fat releases not only energy, but also toxic wastes, called ketones. And these wastes accumulate and slowly poison the body — resulting in such symptoms as nausea, vomiting, and eventually, even diabetic coma. A regular Catch-22.

As if all that weren't bad enough, coincident with ketone poisoning, the diabetic experiences a steady build-up of glucose in the blood. This condition, called hyperglycemia (high blood sugar), produces such familiar diabetic characteristics as exhaustion, frequent urination, crash weight loss, and nervous irritability.

While the short-term effects of hyperglycemia and ketone poisoning can be dealt with through medication, the long-term health consequences are catastrophic for those diabetics who keep eating the standard American diet that's high in fat, and low in fiber and complex-carbohydrates.

What are the long-term complications of diabetes?

For most diabetics, as we've noted, the reverberations from their disease extend far beyond the immediate symptoms of high blood sugar and metabolized fat wastes in the blood. Longtime diabetes sufferers are especially susceptible to diseases of the eyes and kidneys. That's because the cells of those organs (which, by the way, don't require insulin to carry in glucose from the bloodstream) become glucose-saturated when the diabetic's blood sugar levels rise.

In the eyes, these sugar-soaked cells soon begin to petrify, often resulting in cataracts, damage to the retina, and blindness. Injury to the kidneys is equally grievous. There, kidney cells become gummed up by crystallizing sugar and are unable to carry out vital filtration tasks. In time, the kidneys shut down altogether, requiring transplants or hookup to a kidney dialysis machine.

Diabetics are likely to experience other serious ailments as well. Most diabetics suffer from obesity, itself a condition that threatens overall well-being and longevity.

Besides problems with blood glucose, diabetes sufferers also have high levels of fat and cholesterol in the blood. This makes the typical diabetic predisposed for athero-sclerosis (blocked-arteries) and its attendant threat of strokes and heart attacks.

Problems with nervous sensation and circulation also plague diabetics. It's not uncommon for a diabetic to experience infection and gangrene in an extremity and not even know of it until it's too late to do anything but amputate.

Perhaps, the most heartening aspect of diabetes is that its inevitable complications can be almost com-pletely prevented by following a sensible vegetarian diet.

EVENING NEWS WITH TOM BRAKALEE

"Diabetes, a leading killer in the U.S., may have met its conqueror. Studies show that a vegetarian diet could be one of the most effective tools in controlling diabetes."

But how can a vegetarian diet make a difference?

Many researchers feel that a wholefoods vegetarian diet may well be the most critical element in the battle against diabetes. Here's why.

It's been known for over 60 years that those with diabetes are acutely sensitive to the harmful aspects of an unwholesome diet. Since the 1930's, studies have demonstrated that diets high in fat and low in both fiber and complex-carbohydrates exacerbate the diabetic condition. The standard American diet is precisely such an unhealthy regimen.

On the other hand, a vegetarian diet is diabetic-friendly. For several reasons. First, it's naturally high in fiber and complex carbohydrates. Nearly every component of a varied vegetarian diet — whole grains, legumes, fruits, and vegetables — is richly endowed with fiber and complex carbohydrates. And these vital elements are especially critical for diabetics since they act to slow down the release of sugar from the meal into the blood. This action eliminates the problematic glucose highs and lows, permitting blood sugar levels to stabilize. The pancreas then needs only secrete a steady amount of insulin to handle a constant quantity of glucose arriving in the bloodstream.

Second, it's well established that fat adversely affects the diabetic. Such complications as atherosclerosis ("hardening of the arteries"), strokes, and heart attacks are directly related to high fat consumption — especially saturated animal-fat. Also, excess fat in the bloodstream has been shown to be a major cause of the failure of insulin to carry out its proper role in diabetics. While all flesh foods and most animal products are loaded with fat, a vegetarian diet is naturally quite low in fat.

Third, the standard American diet is not only low in fiber and high in fat, it's also chock-full of protein. And a number of studies point out that an excess of protein is particularly harmful for diabetics. That's because an overabundance of protein taxes the kidneys — the organs in charge of getting rid of the protein glut. But a diabetic's kidneys are already nearly worn down by the disease. They don't need more stress. However, a vegetarian diet contains much less protein, thereby giving the diabetic's system a much-needed restorative.

Finally, a vegetarian diet, naturally low in calories (plant foods are bulky, not fattening), permits most obese diabetics to reach their ideal, trim body weight effortlessly. Since obesity is a condition known to aggravate diabetes, a weight-reducing vegetarian diet is yet another weapon in the struggle to eradicate diabetes.

You should be aware, though, that adopting a vegetarian diet will have a powerful — and often sudden — effect on the diabetic's condition. That's why it's critical for a diabetic to work with a registered dietician or other health care provider before making the switch.

Would people with rheumatoid arthritis benefit from adopting a vegetarian diet?

Yes. There's good news for the millions of Americans who suffer from rheumatoid arthritis — unquestionably, the most devastating type of arthritis. Those afflicted with this disease often endure agonizing pain as the joints become inflamed and fingers become contorted and bloated. Frequently, the performance of even the simplest acts cannot be done without anti-inflammatory medication.

Recently, researchers at the University of Oslo (Norway) found that by following a vegetarian diet, rheumatoid arthritis sufferers were able to reduce the pain and swelling associated with the disorder. They experienced far fewer sensitive joints, much less stiffness, and had a much stronger hand grip than their nonvegetarian counterparts.

It's important to note that rheumatoid arthritis is common in the affluent western countries where the excessive consumption of meat and dairy products is the general model. However, the disease is rare in Africa and Asia where traditional diets of whole grains, beans, fruits, and vegetables are still typically emphasized.

Interestingly, when Asians or Africans immigrate to the United States they usually adopt the fatty diet of most

Americans — and that's when rheumatoid arthritis appears for the first time in these people. It would seem that these immigrants are assimilating only too well.

Are the healing effects of a vegetarian diet on rheumatoid arthritis due to the elimination of animal fat?

A fair number of studies link a high, animal-fat diet with rheumatoid arthritis. Note that the typical meat eater's diet is rich in saturated animal fat, whereas a vegetarian diet is devoid of animal fat and naturally low in unsaturated vegetable fat.

Investigators in the aforementioned Norwegian study observed that when the rheumatoid arthritis sufferer consumed a flesh foods diet, the tender joints and swelling were exacerbated. It's known that after eating a meat meal, animal fat quickly enters the bloodstream and sludges the blood to the point of drastically retarding circulation. Immediately, waste products pile up and oxygen flow is reduced. With wastes accumulating in the joints, and little oxygen reaching them, joint-inflammation and swelling are intensified.

But that's not all. The same study found that animal protein, like animal fat, also aggravated the symptoms of rheumatoid arthritis. It was further proof of the harmful effects of a meat-based diet on the arthritic sufferer.

While there are many nutritionists still unable to accept any dietary approach to rheumatoid arthritis, the findings of the Norwegian researchers certainly suggest that a vegetarian diet could play a vital role, along with conventional medical treatment, in greatly reducing the pain and suffering caused by this insidious disease.

Aren't humans inherently meat eaters? After all, meat's been on the menu for a long time.

Despite two million years of eating meat, the human body is biochemically designed by Mother Nature to feast not on flesh, but on plant foods. Our earliest ancestors were vegetarian food gatherers who subsisted on grains, fruits, nuts, and root vegetables. Researchers know this by examining the fossilized feces and teeth of these primeval men and women.

It's believed that a changing climate, eons ago, drastically reduced the plant food supply, forcing these early humans to become hunters. The choice was this: eat meat or starve to death. But even after conditions improved, and the necessity for eating meat diminished, the human fancy for meat was already deeply entrenched. And to our detriment, humans have been eating animal flesh ever since.

What's more, if people really were inborn carnivores, wouldn't you expect them to this day to wolf down chunks of raw, bloody meat? But instead, they roast, sauté, or charbroil animal flesh and then pile on condiments and seasonings to camouflage it. If humans were innate hunters, why do they pay others to kill and dismember domesticated livestock for them? The ranks of vegetarians would swell if each meat eater had to do his or her own killing — to slit an animal's throat or to plunge a steel rod into its brain.

As we've seen, our earliest ancestors became hunters and meat eaters out of necessity — not from any biological or psychological need for animal flesh. Today's meat-hunters don't swing through the trees clutching sharpened rocks. They'd much rather hunt for bargains in the grocery meat department — armed only with a shopping cart.

If humans were meant to be plant eaters, why don't you have a spare stomach, like cows? And what are your canine teeth for if not for ripping meat?

Yours is one of the most frequently repeated arguments used to justify the human fondness for animal flesh. But it's simply not factual to assert that human beings are built like flesh-eating carnivores.

Have you ever considered yourself capable of chasing down a deer and sinking your stubby canines into the poor beast's hindquarters? Those canines that you say were meant to tear meat wouldn't get past the deer's thick skin, let alone have a chance to rip anything. Human canine teeth don't often get mistaken for the true canines found in all carnivorous animals. Those teeth are long, pointed, and razor sharp. They don't have any trouble piercing the toughest hide.

Human beings have a mouthful of flat teeth, implanted in an exceptionally mobile jaw that can move from side to side. Perfect for grinding and chewing grains, nuts, and other plant foods. Whereas, the carnivore's jaw, crammed with knife-like teeth, can only open and close like a pair of scissors. Good for tearing and swallowing large chunks of flesh. With their relatively immobile jaws, carnivores hardly bother to chew their food at all.

People have large, well-developed salivary glands that secrete an alkaline saliva for digesting plant foods. On the other hand, the carnivore has diminutive salivary glands which produce an acidic saliva — suitable only for a superficial degree of meat digestion in the mouth. In humans, digestion earnestly begins in the mouth; in carnivores it's in the gut.

Mother Nature gave carnivores a short, smooth, and simple digestive system for a critical reason. Since dead flesh decays swiftly it must be rapidly digested and expelled before the toxic wastes and bacteria accumulate and cause serious infection. To aid in this process, the carnivore's stomach secretes copious amounts of potent hydrochloric acid — at least 10 times the quantity found in humans.

Since plant foods take a long time to be digested, and are relatively free of the toxins, wastes, and microorganisms found in decaying flesh, the human digestive system has a completely different design than that of the carnivore. Your intestines are long, very long — running 30 feet or more in length. Grooved, ridged, and full of twists and turns, the human gut is quite efficient at absorbing plant food nutrients — even without the benefit of an extra stomach like that found in cows and horses. Recall, that the carnivore's bowels, in contrast, are smooth. This feature effectively prevents putrefying flesh from becoming lodged in a fold or crease.

And while there are plenty of remaining physiological and anatomical dissimilarities between humans and carnivores, I think you get the picture: Mother Nature never intended human beings to consume rotting meat (face it, from roadkill to the meat just put out by the butcher — all dead flesh is at some stage of putrefaction).

Chapter 3

Economics, Ecology, and Ethics

Why is meat eating considered a wasteful practice?

You be the judge. Consider what it takes to produce just one pound of beef. After about six months of foraging on public grazing lands, a typical beef steer is shipped to the feedlot for fattening. Weighing in between 700 and 800 pounds, the animal will spend the next three months devouring about three-fourths of a ton of plant proteins (chiefly grains and soybeans).

At the end of this binge, the steer will weigh about 1,000 pounds. Although it has gained several hundred pounds on the feedlot, only about 100 pounds of that increase is edible beef. The rest is bone, hide, hair, and other inedibles that will never grace anyone's dinner table.

So after consuming 1,500 pounds of nourishing beans and grains, the animal has shown a paltry net increase of 100 pounds of edible meat. That works out to 15 pounds of valuable plant proteins being used up to create each pound of beef. Multiply this waste by countless millions of feedlot animals, and you begin to see the staggering quantity of food that's squandered to support a meat-centered diet.

Nutritionists estimate that if Americans ate just 10 percent less meat, there'd be enough grains and beans saved to feed tens of millions of people. It's especially tragic to consider that in the time it took you to read this sentence, three children starved to death somewhere in the world.

Well, couldn't you save all that food by simply eliminating feedlots and allowing animals to graze in pastures and rangelands instead?

I'm afraid there's not enough vegetation in all the grazing lands combined to adequately fatten up the colossal number of animals slaughtered each year to satisfy this country's craving for meat.

Besides, most of America's rangelands, particularly in the west, are already so seriously overgrazed that over four billion tons of precious top soil are lost each year. In fact, no other human activity destroys more land and vegetation than does cattle grazing.

But how can so much devastation be caused by gentle sheep and cattle grazing peacefully on the range? These animals — "hooved locusts" according to the late naturalist John Muir — eat every speck of vegetation they can. When the last blade of grass has been put away, the livestock move on to denude other greener pastures.

They leave behind trampled, arid, hard soil — barren as the lunar landscape. The coming rains aren't able to get through the packed soil to replenish the underground water supplies. And with no plants to anchor the soil, the winds have no trouble carrying off this vital resource.

Why doesn't the government do something about this? It's already doing plenty. Federal and state governments routinely lease out hundreds of millions of acres of public lands to private ranching conglomerates — all at below-market rates. In effect, your tax dollars subsidize the trashing of America's vast rangeland. But that's not all that government funds are used for.

What else?

For brutally exterminating all animals that compete with grazing livestock for grass and water. Tens of millions of dollars of federal money are spent each year to trap, shoot, or poison millions of birds and other creatures that are considered just plain nuisances.

Although wild horses have not been shown to have any effect on grazing livestock, thousands of untamed horses are captured each year by federal game wardens and dispatched to slaughterhouses. Next stop for these noble beasts: dogfood.

Predatory animals fare no better. Whether shot at from low-flying aircraft, allowed to die slowly in painful leghold traps, blown up by explosives, torched, or torn apart by packs of vicious dogs — these predators are not permitted to interfere with the interests of the cattle industry. Thus, such "threats" to livestock as grizzly bears, cougars, gray wolves, foxes, mountain lions, eagles, and hawks are being systematically destroyed to insure the uninterrupted flow of cheap burgers to America's fast food outlets.

I've heard that it takes several hundred gallons of water to produce just one pound of steak. How can that be?

Brace yourself. It's far worse than that. A number of researchers have concluded that the production of each pound of beef requires the use of an astonishing 2,500 gallons of fresh water. In other words, that's two and one-half million gallons for each half-ton steer — enough water to fill four Olympic-sized pools! And enough water, as Newsweek noted some time ago, to float a warship!

In every step of the way in meat production — such as in irrigating feed crops, in carrying off the immense wastes created by feedlots, and in processing slaughtered steers — enormous quantities of water are consumed. It's been estimated that the lion's share of all the water used in the United States goes solely to raising livestock.

And in order to grow forage crops to feed hundreds of millions of livestock animals each year, irrigation water is pumped out of deep, pure ground water sources, called aquifers. In fact, billions more gallons of water are pumped out each day from America's aquifers than Mother Nature can replace. Scientists predict that at this rate of depletion, within your own lifetime, entire aquifers, some as large in area as several states combined, will completely dry up due exclusively to overpumping for livestock production.

What can be done about it? Well, studies show that vegetarians require only one-third as much water to grow their food than that needed by meat eaters. And vegans (vegetarians who consume neither dairy products nor eggs) need only one-fifteenth the water that their meat-eating counterparts do.

Is there anything else that's wasteful about meat production?

Yes, there certainly is. Meat production consumes much more energy than does a vegetarian diet of plant-based foods. Studies show that it takes over 40 times more fuel energy to produce beef than it does an equal amount of grains and beans.

In order to grow and harvest the massive quantities of feed for the hundreds of millions of livestock animals, astonishing amounts of energy are called for. Picture all those millions of tractors, combines, trucks, pumps, and other specialized machinery running through millions of gallons of fuel each day.

Imagine thousands of factory farms, with their huge cavernous "barns" crammed with cows, calves, chickens, sheep and pigs. Tremendous amounts of energy are gobbled up to heat and cool these structures, as well as to bring feed to the animals and to carry off their wastes.

Yet even greater quantities of energy are spent in processing, packaging, refrigerating, transporting, storing, and preparing the meat for the marketplace.

You've already seen that 2,500 gallons of water, plus 15 pounds of soybeans and grains are used to produce a single pound of meat. Get ready for another shocker. In addition, it takes the energy equivalent of an entire gallon of gas to get a single pound of meat to the dinner table.

And since the typical American consumes over 200 pounds of meat each year, that's 200 gallons of fuel used annually by each man, woman, and child to support the meat habit. For the country, that works out to over 50 billion gallons of fuel per annum just to produce meat.

Even if the average American were to cut back meat consumption by just a few pounds each week, the fuel savings to the nation would be immense — and felt around the globe. It could even free the U.S. from its chronic dependency on unstable sources of foreign oil. And such a modest reduction would do wonders to reduce the pollution created by a meat-centered diet.

But how does eating meat pollute the environment?

Any way you look at it, the production of meat is not an environmentally-friendly undertaking. In fact, some of this country's most serious pollution problems can be traced to the doorsteps of the livestock industry.

Livestock animals, packed in by the tens of thousands on barren feedlots, generate hundreds of millions of tons of manure each year. Unfortunately, there's no way to keep these wastes from running off into America's rivers, streams, and lakes. And when vast quantities of manure are disposed of on soil, nitrates from the waste material trickle down and adulterate the groundwater below. In some places around the country, the groundwater supplies are so poisoned as to be beyond any use.

Slaughterhouse wastes are another source of water contamination. Meat-packers and other livestock processors discharge millions of pounds of grease, blood, intestinal waste, and other solid matter into sewer systems that empty into the great waterways of this land.

The environment is damaged in other ways by livestock production. Each day, several hundred million American cows belch and flatulate substantial amounts of methane gas, a byproduct of feed digestion. And methane is one of the gases that contributes to global warming. Scientists are concerned that even modest temperature increases could have a catastrophic impact on animals, plants, and crops around the world. It's even possible that the polar icecaps could defrost, causing the oceans to rise and deluge coastal areas.

Carbon dioxide, another incidental product of the cattle industry, plays an especially deleterious role in causing the "greenhouse effect" and the resultant rise in atmospheric temperatures. Recall that factory farming and large-scale agriculture (that chiefly grows livestock feed) require inordinate amounts of energy — which are obtained by burning fossil fuels. And the burning of such fuels releases large quantities of carbon dioxide. This gas escapes into the atmosphere where it works in tandem with methane (from cows) to trap solar heat.

Further exacerbating the problem caused by these "man made" gases, vast forestlands are cleared to make room for grazing land, feedlots, and farmland on which to grown livestock feed. Destroying forests is sad for many reasons. It is especially so, in light of this discussion, because trees have the ability to absorb carbon dioxide and other polluting gases.

Ironically, a meat-centered diet not only creates life-threatening global pollution, it also eliminates a potential remedy.

Aren't farm animals generally treated humanely before they're slaughtered?

Most people have a vague notion that animals raised for food spend their lives grazing in green pastures and wandering freely about the farmyard. That may have been the case in the distant past, but today's farm animals — pigs, chickens, dairy cows, calves, and beef cattle — are all raised on highly-automated factory farms where they're considered as nothing more than meat-making machines.

Nearly all these animals spend their whole lives tightly confined in small cages or boxes. They never get to feel a breeze, or see green pastures, sunshine, or life outside their windowless, factory buildings.

Furthermore, every aspect of their lives is controlled by the factory manager. Natural functions are not left up to Mother Nature. Animals are pumped with hormones to radically boost development; antibiotics and other drugs are administered to contend with the terrible diseases that proliferate in these unnatural, unhealthy settings. Some animals are kept in darkness most of the time to keep them calm; others are exposed to uninterrupted, artificial light to encourage productivity. They eat, sleep, become pregnant, and die whenever the manager decides.

Imprisoned, drugged, manipulated, exploited, often mutilated (to prevent them from pecking, clawing, or biting their cellmates), farm animals are treated so abominably as to be denied even an iota of enjoyment before being slaughtered.

Even though all farm animals suffer under similarly harsh conditions, two animals in particular seem to have it much worse than the others.

What do you mean by that?

Probably no factory farm animal suffers a crueler fate than veal calves. Removed from their mothers shortly after birth, the calves are placed in small, narrow wooden crates and denied any exercise, sunshine, fresh air, or contact with other animals. Calves are intentionally placed in tight confinement (their heads chained to the stalls, without even enough room to move, stretch, or lie down) since any exercise would develop muscles and make their meat less tender.

To produce the pale flesh that fetches high prices from gourmets everywhere, veal farmers feed the calves a high-calorie, iron-deficient, milky porridge that's laced with antibiotics and other drugs. Also, this diet insures that these animals will experience rapid weight gain and remain healthy enough (barely!) to eke out their 100-day lives until slaughter. However, this all-liquid diet, completely devoid of the roughage that all cud-chewing mammals biologically require, causes serious intestinal disorders and diarrhea for the animals' entire lives. Locked in their crates, calves are forced to stand in their own excrement 24 hours a day.

Finally, these baby animals, separated from parental nurturing, are deprived of their strong natural urges to nurse from their mothers. Unable to do so, the frustrated, pathetic calves repeatedly suck on any object that they can reach.

Mercifully, this inhumane treatment comes to an end barely three months from the time the calves first open their eyes. Their only trip out of prison, however, is the one to the slaughterhouse. When the doors are swung open, and the neck-chains removed, many calves are too weak to walk. They must be dragged out. Some struggle for that first step, only to collapse in death from overexertion.

What other farm animal is treated especially badly?

As with veal calves, chickens live nasty, brutal, and shortened lives in crowded and cruel imprisonment. In order to maximize profits, chicken factory farms have become highly specialized — with "broilers" (chickens raised for meat) found exclusively on some farms, and "layers" (chickens that lay eggs) on others.

Broiler chickens are raised in large, windowless sheds where thousands of birds (flocks can exceed 50,000) stand around in their foul-smelling excrement and compete for enough room just to turn around. The extreme overcrowding and stress of factory farm life make the chickens aggressive — and cannibalistic. To solve the problem, chickens are debeaked, a frightfully painful procedure in which the bone and sensitive tissue of their beaks are severed with a red-hot knife.

Since broiler bedding (typically wood shavings) is reused many times, the chickens are continuously exposed to diseases and parasites. And without access to sunlight, fresh air, or exercise, these birds are at great risk of succumbing to the many epidemics that sweep the chicken sheds. In response, broilers are fed meal that's laced with antibiotics. It's cheaper to raise the birds in filth and use drugs to ward off disease, than it is to reduce overcrowding and give birds access to the grass, dirt, and sunshine found in the natural world. In any event, after 60 days of life, (about 10 years before the end of their natural lifespan) broilers are dispatched to the slaughter-house.

In contrast, egg-laying chickens spend their entire lives (about 15 months), in tiny, 12-by-18 inch wire-mesh cages that are stacked vertically to the ceiling. With five birds in each enclosure, there's no room to walk or even flap a wing. As with broilers, egg-layers are painfully debeaked to keep them from pecking and eating their fellow cellmates. These birds are fed chemically-laced feed to counter the effects of the feces that continuously drips over them from the stacked cages above.

And after their egg-laying days have ended, the thoroughly exhausted chickens are slaughtered, then delivered to the processors to be made into soup, frozen food, and pet food.

Aren't there any factory farm animals at all that receive decent treatment?

Sadly, no. It would go against what factory farming is all about. I'll explain. Factory farm operators consider the humane treatment of their animals as an obstacle to maximizing productivity and profit. If animals were allowed to roam a bit — to have even a little space to call their own — costs for land and buildings would increase. Automated operations would be impossible if the animals weren't tightly confined. Additional employees would be required; labor costs would escalate.

Furthermore, un-confined animals would move about and burn up calories. Weight gains would be slower and more feed would be required. Costs would rise. Besides, exercise has a nasty side effect. It makes meat tougher; and less tender meat won't fetch premium prices in the supermarket.

All factory farms are alike in this respect: They view animals as nothing more than machines that must be gotten as big as possible in the shortest time for the least amount of money. The animals' feelings or biological needs are irrelevant. And any procedure or treatment that promotes a fatter bottom line, however horrific, is considered reasonable.

Recently, I passed a truck on the highway that was wall-to-wall with cattle. How bad is it for animals in transit?

There is no let up in the brutality, even for livestock being transported. At some point in their lives most farm animals are shipped to auction yards, feedlots, or slaughterhouses. They're crammed tightly into trucks or trailers and hauled long distances without food or water. The animals can be boxed up for days, in abnormal heat or cold, without an opportunity to move about and stretch their legs. In fact, they can be so compressed that livestock in the center will occasionally suffocate. And animals that somehow manage to lose their footing can be crushed to death.

Aside from the trip itself, livestock experience abuse when boarding the trucks, and later when exiting. Animals fresh from factory farms are fat and in poor muscular condition. Their wobbily legs can hardly support any movements. Which makes it a frightening, bewildering affair to be forced to run up and down steep, often slippery ramps. And to get them to move more quickly, the animals are repeatedly hit and kicked by the overseers.

Livestock too weak or injured to disembark on their own are dragged off the trucks with ropes or chains attached to their necks or legs. Crippled, diseased animals judged unfit for human consumption are moved out of sight and dumped in a pile — forced to wait for days to die or be killed. (Later, they'll be made into pet food.) In extreme weather, it's not uncommon for these hapless animals to be frozen to the ground, still alive.

At least, aren't livestock humanely slaughtered?

There's nothing humane about the process at all. Typically, the cattle, calves, or pigs just arriving at the slaughterhouse have come a long distance, standing shoulder to shoulder the whole way. They're confused by the trip, exhausted, and in many cases, quite ill. They haven't been fed for at least a day as it would make bad economic sense to feed an animal a final meal that won't be digested and turned into marketable meat before slaughter.

And while slaughterhouse workers may not be innately sadistic people, the pressures of their grisly work cause many of them to be harsh with the animals. Consequently, they pour down a torrent of angry shouts, slaps, and punches upon the disoriented livestock. Assembled by the hundreds or thousands, the terrified animals must wait outside the slaughterhouse for their turn to enter and be put to death.

As they hear the anguished cries of animals that have preceded them, the livestock are gripped by the specter of death. It is now only by severe blows and electric shocks that the animals grudgingly make their way into the killing rooms.

Contrary to what you may think, there are no mandated humane methods of killing animals. Slaughterhouse operators may choose any means (usually the cheapest!), however barbaric or cold-blooded. In most slaughterhouses, the terror-stricken animals are first rendered unconscious by a blow to the head (often a steel bolt is fired into the brain), or by an electrical shock, or by another technique before they're shackled, hoisted, and stabbed repeatedly in the chest and neck in order to sever the major arteries. With blood spurting out of numerous wounds, the animals quickly bleed to death.

Even more shocking, a number of slaughterhouses do not first stun the animals. Instead, they're shackled, jacked up, and pierced while fully conscious (and in great pain from having their half-ton bodies suspended just by a hind leg). These poor creatures are stabbed and bled to death while wide-awake!

In a similar fashion, chickens are not knocked out before being killed. With their legs shackled, the birds are hung upside down on an overhead moving chain and guided toward spinning, razor-sharp blades that cut their throats (and nearly decapitate them). The chickens then are passed through tubs of seething hot water to loosen their feathers. However, because some birds squirm or are irregular in size, they miss the cutting blades entirely. It is to their final misfortune that they enter the cauldrons of boiling water — alive and struggling.

Why worry about the treatment of farm animals? How do we know they're even capable of suffering or experiencing pleasure?

Researchers have long known that most animals have nervous systems and brain components that are quite similar to those found in humans. Meaning that animals are able to process pain impulses in much the same way as you can.

Animals react to dangerous situations as people do — they try to flee, they cry out in pain if hurt, they bleed, and they try to cradle and soothe the injured part. And just like you, animals can see, smell, hear, touch, and taste. Although they don't speak any human language, they're able to communicate — even to think and reason — in ways that human beings don't yet comprehend.

When frightened or terribly excited, both animals and people secrete adrenaline, as well as experience a faster heart beat, higher blood pressure, and rapid breathing. All creatures, human and otherwise, learn to stay away from harmful situations, and return to pleasurable ones.

It should be clear from this discussion that animals have at least one desire: to live. Furthermore, they show an awareness of both pain and pleasure. In other words, they possess the ability to suffer. And because of that capacity, they have the right not to be harmed.

From time immemorial, sages have been warning that to disregard the suffering brought upon animals not only stains the human spirit, it also makes it easier to direct that inhumanity — at one's fellow human beings.

How do you defend killing plants? Don't they have feelings, too?

The issue here is the capacity to feel pain and to suffer. It's believed that plants are incapable of experiencing pain since they lack a nervous system. How can you be sure that plants don't feel pain? Static life forms, namely plants, have no way of benefitting from such a capacity.

For example, if something injures you, you immediately feel pain and usually react with fight or flight. You stand up and give battle, or you get away fast. Since plants can't run away or actively defend themselves, Mother Nature would have had no reason to permit plants to know pain. It would have been unkind and cruel to allow plants to suffer without giving them the power to do something about it. On the other hand, such mobile creatures as humans and animals can feel pain — and owe their survival to that capability.

Yet, plants are alive, and may even possess a certain sensitivity not yet understood by humans. Still, it must be recognized that these living things have to be killed if humans are to survive. And to cause the least suffering in the world, only as few plants as necessary should be eaten.

Recall that livestock are fed enormous amounts of plant food for each pound of edible meat produced. Thus, meat eaters indirectly kill a far greater number of plants than do vegetarians. Not only that, a meat-centered diet is responsible for the slaughter of over five billion farm animals each year in the U.S. — creatures we know for sure that are capable of suffering.

Isn't a vegetarian who uses animal products guilty of hypocrisy?

That would hinge on one's motives for becoming a vegetarian. If it's for health reasons, for example, it wouldn't be inconsistent for a vegetarian to wear leather or fur and to use other animal products. On the other hand, if a vegan (a vegetarian who eschews animals products because of the abuse, exploitation, and slaughter of animals) were to use animal byproducts you could certainly call that a contradiction.

Okay, what about dairy products and eggs? Well, there's nothing hypocritical about a vegetarian eating eggs or drinking milk. Recall that a vegetarian is one who consumes no meat, fish, or poultry. Nothing in that definition about dairy products, eggs, or leather, for example. Besides, animals are not slaughtered to obtain eggs and milk.

Vegans are quick to point out, however, that dairy cows and egg-laying hens are harshly exploited on factory farms and then slaughtered after they're no longer productive.

However, despite the legitimacy of that vegan assertion, it's important to keep in mind that a vegetarian lifestyle, even one that includes dairy products, eggs, leather, and other animal byproducts, is a godsend (in general) for farm animals everywhere — as well as for the health of one's self and planet. That's because the problems caused by a meat-based diet would be greatly minimized if farm animals were raised only for the production of milk, eggs, leather and other byproducts. The number of animals that would be exploited and slaughtered on that account would be a drop in the bucket compared to the billions of farm animals butchered for food each year in America.

In fact, even non-vegetarians could help reduce the unnecessary brutality and carnage on factory farms and slaughterhouses (and benefit themselves and the earth) simply by cutting down on their own consumption of meat.

If everyone became vegetarians, what about the jobs lost in the meat industry? And wouldn't farm animals overwhelm the planet?

Rest assured, a mass conversion to vegetarianism is not likely to happen overnight. It would be a very slow process, at best. During this transition period, meat producers gradually could shift to large-scale production of plant-based foods like tofu, beanburgers, soy milk, vegetarian chili and stew, soy ice cream and yogurt, and many others. And a part of the vast sums of money saved by all Americans because of reduced health costs — recall that a meat-centered diet is responsible for heart disease, many cancers, osteoporosis, and numerous other ailments — could be earmarked for job creation and worker retraining.

America's farmers, with their fertile boundless fields, could benefit handsomely from the changeover to vegetarianism. In a vegetarian world, the demand for soy and other plant-foods would be phenomenal; and this nation's farmers could supply the mountains of beans and other plant foods for the myriad of processing plants that would spring up to handle the burgeoning domestic and world demand for America's vegetarian foodstuffs.

And what about the threat of a glut of uneaten farm animals engulfing the earth? It can't happen. Why? Because domestic farm animals exclusively owe their existence to the meat industry that raises billions of them annually for slaughter. As more people became vegetarians, the demand for meat would plummet, and the meat industry would breed less animals.

In time, farm animals could be left to fend for themselves; some would make out fine, others would struggle to keep from becoming extinct. But, like all animals (except humans), they would adjust their numbers in accordance with the conditions around them.

Chapter 4

Pregnancy, Children, Athletes, and Pets

Can a vegetarian diet provide all the nutrients necessary for a healthy pregnancy?

Despite the fact that vegetarians eat far better than the rest of the population, pregnancy is a special time that makes even many vegetarians nervous. However, studies have long shown that pregnant vegetarians have hearty pregnancies and healthy, normal babies. There's nothing in the medical literature that even remotely suggests that pregnant vegetarians who eat a wide variety of whole, natural foods are at greater risk of nutrient insufficiencies than pregnant meat eaters.

A number of doctors and dieticians feel that it's not necessary for a vegetarian to follow any carefully-monitored dietary plan during pregnancy. Simply by satisfying her hunger with an assortment of healthful, unrefined foods, a pregnant vegetarian will be certain of getting all the nourishment to ensure a fine pregnancy and baby.

Of course, one of the first things a pregnant vegetarian should do is find a physician, dietician, or other health care professional who is supportive of the vegetarian approach to pregnancy.

At least during pregnancy shouldn't a vegetarian play it safe and include some meat in the diet?

Not at all. There's no scientific evidence whatsoever that eating meat makes it more likely that you'll have a successful pregnancy and healthy baby. In fact, considering that animal flesh harbors residues of growth hormones, antibiotics, bacteria, and pesticides, and is loaded with saturated fat and cholesterol — shouldn't a meat eater play it safe and discontinue eating meat during pregnancy?

Alarmingly, studies show that harmful residues and toxins found in meat, poultry, and fish are taken in by the rapidly developing fetus, affecting it in ways not yet understood. After all, why take a chance with meat when a vegetarian diet already contains all the nutrients found in flesh foods?

What are a pregnant vegetarian's nutritional needs, anyway?

In order to gain the recommended amount of weight, pregnant vegetarians (and nonvegetarians, too) are advised to eat an additional 300 calories each day. This shouldn't be difficult, because as the pregnancy advances, a vegetarian's appetite will naturally increase — so there's no need to make a conscious effort to eat more. And the unsurpassed way to get these extra calories is by eating a wide assortment of whole grain products, legumes, fruits, and vegetables.

As most nutritionists point out, pregnancy does not grant a free license to wolf down excessively fatty or sugary junk foods to cover those 300 daily surplus calories. Doing so would rob the developing fetus of the vital nutrients it needs. The best advice during pregnancy is to wisely use up those extra 300 calories each day, making certain that they're packed with nutrition — because all mothers-to-be need lots more nutrients at this weighty time in their lives.

Good advice. But could you be more specific about those key nutrients?

Certainly. All pregnant women require (besides the extra calories) more of these three essential nutrients: protein, iron, and calcium. What are these nutrients needed for? Read on.

Protein is necessary to build new tissue in both mother and baby. Most experts advise that around 60 to 70 grams of protein should be eaten each day during pregnancy. While that may seem like lots (after all, that is almost 70 percent more than what's recommended for non-pregnant women), protein is not that hard to find. Look for it in such plant-based foods as whole grains, beans, tofu, tempeh, soy milk, nuts, seeds, and green vegetables.

Iron plays a critical role in forming the baby's blood supply and is also needed to help increase the mother's own blood volume. If the mother's diet is iron-deficient, her stored-up iron will be tapped for duty — and she can become anemic as a result. So, should mothers-to-be take iron supplements? Many nutrition experts actually discourage them, suggesting instead that iron-rich, whole foods like leafy green vegetables, dried fruits, nuts, seeds, raisins, beans, molasses, and whole grains be eaten to supply the necessary iron.

But, to play it safe, you might want to have your iron level checked several times during pregnancy. If the readings turn up low, iron supplements could be called for by your health care provider. Otherwise, eating a varied vegetarian diet will provide all the iron you need. And remember, you can dramatically increase absorption of iron by including vitamin C-rich foods along with the iron-rich ones.

The vital element responsible for the development of bones and teeth in the fetus is calcium. And contrary to popular belief, milk is not the best place to find calcium. For several reasons. First, many people simply cannot digest milk. Second, dairy products are high in protein, which, studies show, actually works against calcium absorption. Finally, many plant foods are abundantly endowed with a form of calcium that's more easily absorbed by your body than animal-derived calcium.

Therefore, instead of drinking plenty of milk, pregnant women would be wise to get all the calcium they need from such particularly rich sources as leafy green vegetables, broccoli, beans, nuts, seeds, tofu (made with calcium salts — check the package label), figs, molasses, apricots, and dates.

In addition to protein, iron, and calcium, there are several other important nutrients that must be taken in greater measure during pregnancy.

Which ones?

A pregnant woman also needs to increase her regular intake of folic acid, zinc, and vitamins B12 and D. These micro-nutrients are responsible for a host of vital functions affecting the health of both the mother and developing fetus.

An emphasis on a varied, vegetarian diet — whole grains, legumes, dark green and yellow vegetables (especially leafy greens), nuts, seeds, and fruits — will supply ample amounts of zinc and folic acid; but something extra has to be done concerning vitamins B12 and D.

For those vegetarians who avoid eggs and dairy products (vegans) a reliable source of vitamin B12 is a must during pregnancy. And while B12 is not found in any plant-based foods, vegans can get all that they need from

B12 fortified nutritional yeasts, fortified cereals, and fortified "fake meats." But, to be absolutely certain of getting enough vitamin B12, a number of nutritionists suggest that vegan mothers-to-be regularly include B12 supplement pills in their diets.

As with B12, a plant-based diet does not supply any vitamin D. So, many vegetarians get their vitamin D from eggs or from milk that's been fortified with this vitamin. On the other hand, a number of vegetarians refuse to drink vitamin D fortified milk when they learn that this vitamin is actually obtained from fish-liver oils prior to being added to milk at the processing plant. Fortunately, there's a natural way to get vitamin D without resorting to animal products.

Which way is that? From sunlight. Vitamin D is produced by your own body following exposure to the sun. Pregnant vegans are advised to expose at least their faces and hands (and more, if weather permits) to the sun for 15 to 30 minutes at a time, several times a week. This should supply all the vitamin D that's needed during pregnancy. However, if a vegan finds it impossible to get even this modest amount of sun exposure, it might be prudent to confer with a health care provider regarding the necessity of taking vegetarian formula vitamin D supplements.

VEGETARIANS AT PLAY

Is a vegetarian diet fully adequate for active, growing children?

Of course it is. In fact, varied, wholefood vegetarian and vegan (without dairy and eggs) diets provide greater amounts of useful vitamins and minerals than does the typical meat based diet. After all, any nutrients found in meat and other animal products were originally obtained by the animals from the plant foods they ate. Vegetarians get their life-sustaining nutrients directly from the source, without having them processed through animal flesh first.

Vegetarian kids can get all the protein they need for building healthy bodies by eating a variety of whole grains, beans, green vegetables, nuts, and seeds. The water-soluble vitamins can be picked up by consuming green leafy vegetables, whole grains, beans, nuts, seeds, and fruits. On the other hand, the fat-soluble vitamins are well-provided by vegetables (especially such yellow vegetables like yams, carrots, and squash), whole grains, vegetable oils, nuts, and fruits.

What about minerals? No problem on a vegetarian diet. Leafy greens, whole grains, nuts, seeds, sea vegetables, and many other plant foods are teeming with all the minerals a growing body needs.

Numerous studies show that youngsters raised on a plant-based diet not only grow and develop normally, they are also much less likely as adults to be stricken with heart disease and certain cancers than are nonvegetarian children. It is certainly no exaggeration to assert that a vegetarian diet is the best start in life any child could get.

But aren't children raised on a vegetarian diet measurably smaller than their meat-eating peers?

Not so, according to the experts. Over the years, both the American Dietetic Association and the National Academy of Sciences have issued favorable position papers recognizing that vegetarian infants and children have no growth problems.

Several years ago, investigators at Loma Linda University in California conducted a study which confirmed what vegetarian parents have known for a long time —

that vegetarian children do indeed thrive on a meatless diet. In that study, the heights and weights of about 2,500 Seventh-Day Adventist youngsters (who generally followed an ovo-lacto vegetarian diet) and meat-eating children were compared. It was found that while vegetarian and nonvegetarian girls showed no consequential statistical differences, vegetarian boys were, on average, nearly an inch taller than boys following a meat-based diet.

Another recent study involved children raised from birth on a vegan diet. It concluded that vegan children were not significantly different, in terms of weight and height, from youngsters in the general population.

And while vegetarian and nonvegetarian kids of similar age seem to grow up to around the same size, a vegetarian diet enables that growth to be slower and more evenly spaced out over the child's developing years.

Why's that important?

Because rapid maturity has been linked to a variety of cancers. Whereas, a slower rate of development, as typically experienced by vegetarian children, is associated with a lower risk of cancer.

Many health professionals are alarmed by the unusually early sexual maturation and menstruation found in young women who follow a meat-based diet. It's a frightening development because there's ample evidence indicating that women who began menstruating early in life — before age 13 — are at a much greater risk of developing breast cancer than are women whose menstrual period first occurred in their later teen years.

What's behind this rapid blossoming? None other than the excessive consumption of meat. More precisely:

fat. All flesh foods are packed with fat. And it's long been known that a high-fat diet raises the levels of the hormones responsible for sexual development. On the other hand, vegetarian youngsters eat much less fat, mature slower, start menstruating later — and have vastly lower rates of cancer than their meat-eating counterparts.

I've heard that heart disease starts in childhood. How can that be?

The fat-rich standard American diet not only raises children's blood cholesterol levels, it also leaves fatty deposits in their arteries. Autopsy studies on over 1,500 teenagers killed in accidents revealed the presence of hardened patches of fat already clogging up their youthful arteries.

A recent study of California elementary school children showed that an appallingly high 40 percent of the youngsters had blood cholesterol levels measuring in the moderate to high-risk range. On the other hand, a study of young vegetarians in Massachusetts revealed that these children had low blood cholesterol and were not considered to be at risk for developing heart disease later in life.

These and other studies indicate that vegetarian youngsters have clean coronary arteries because a plant-derived diet is, among other things, naturally low in fat and high in fiber — wholesome factors missing from a meat-based diet.

Just a minute. Don't kids need more fat than adults to avoid stunted growth?

It's true that developing children need fat in order to absorb vitamins and grow properly. But with most adults in America getting a shocking 50 percent of their calories from fat, no sane nutritionist would advise parents to feed their children more fat than that. In fact, recognizing that heart disease starts in childhood, most nutrition experts (including the U.S. Government) recommend that young-sters over the age of two receive a fat intake of only 20 to 30 percent of total calories.

Children over two years old have digestive systems mature enough to get all the fat they need from a variety of vegetarian foods, such as tofu, nuts and seeds (and the butters made from them), beans, avocados, soy milk, and vegetable oils. And combining these fatty foods with whole grains, fruits, and vegetables will create a well-balanced diet able to meet all of a growing child's nutritional needs.

In determining how much fat a child should be receiving, a parent could keep detailed records of how many grams of fat are eaten each day. Or, a simpler way to go about this would be for children who are overweight and sedentary to be given less fatty foods, while those kids who are underweight and very active could have a little more fat included in their diets.

So far, this discussion has dealt with children over the age of two. The rules are very different for infants under two. They really do require a high-fat diet — which is why Mother Nature endowed breast milk with a fat content of nearly 50 percent. Many health professionals advise that infants should be breastfed for the first two years. But, if that's not possible, it's recommend that a fortified, soy-based formula be fed to infants. Three such formulas which contain no animal products are Prosobee, Soyalac, and Isomil.

Before choosing a formula, however, it might not be a bad idea to discuss this issue with your health care provider. Furthermore, invaluable advice concerning the first solid vegetarian foods that infants and children should be fed can be found in the following, highly-recommended books: *Pregnancy, Children, and the Vegan Diet; Vegan Nutrition: Pure and Simple;* and *Simply Vegan* (see Resources).

GUESS WHICH ONES ARE VEGETARIANS!

Have there been other studies regarding the health of children raised on vegetarian diets?

You bet. It's already been noted that vegetarian children have cleaner arteries and lower blood cholesterol levels than their meat-eating peers. And vegetarians grow up with a much lower risk of falling victim to heart disease and cancer. They also develop and bloom without any problems. But that's not all.

While a vegetarian diet cannot automatically guarantee a lean, trim body (remember that dairy products and eggs are fat-rich animal products), numerous studies report very little obesity in vegetarian children as opposed to the distressing levels of fatness found in the school-age population as a whole.

A study of over 1,200 young people showed that vegetarian youngsters have healthier teeth than nonvegetarian children. Researchers really couldn't explain why so few of the vegetarians showed signs of tooth decay while nearly half of the nonvegetarian kids had dental caries.

Another study, reported in *The Journal of the American Dietetic Association*, concerned mental, rather than physical health. Vegetarian youngsters were given standard IQ tests — and the results were yet another confirmation of the superiority of a vegetarian diet. The vegetarian children scored significantly higher — nearly 20 percent above the average — and were found to be mentally one year older than their actual, physical ages.

However, health studies aside, most youngsters are more concerned with their personal appearance than with cancer or living to be 100. Health professionals (and vegetarian parents, too) observe that a vegetarian diet offers more than just health benefits. They report that vegetarian kids are more emotionally steady, tend to be less gloomy and sullen, have more endurance, have healthier complexions, get sick less often, and do better in school than their meat-eating classmates.

Others, including John McDougall, M.D., point out that youngsters who consume lots of flesh foods have bad breath and stinky body odor, get pimples, have greasy skin, and aren't as competitive in sports because they just don't have the stamina they could have on a vegetarian diet.

Don't athletes really need to eat meat to build muscle?

It's been known for over a century that athletes do not need meat to "beef-up" their muscles. Yet, this myth persists; and coaches all across the nation continue to advise their athletes to wolf down extravagant amounts of flesh foods and dairy products.

To set the record straight, all the nutrients that you require to build muscle can be found in plant-derived foods. Whole grains, beans, peas, lentils, and vegetables have all the protein and essential amino acids needed to turn any 98 pound weakling into an Arnold Schwarzenegger.

But what's all this obsession about protein, anyway? As a matter of fact, even hard-working athletes like weightlifters, runners, soccer players, cyclists, cross country skiers, and swimmers actually need just a little bit more protein than the typical, sedentary couch potato. What? That's because the daily diet (vegetarian and nonvegetarian, alike) already provides a lot more protein than you actually need. Studies reveal that even vegetarians eat twice as much protein as needed — while meat eaters eat an incredible four times more than is required.

And as we've noted, excessive protein in the diet is unhealthy — it can leach calcium out of your bones and weaken your kidneys. (Recall that the kidneys have to work overtime to filter out the overload of toxins and acids that gets dumped in the blood as a result of too much protein in the diet.) Also, something for athletes to consider: Too much protein can lead to dehydration and debilitating intestinal disorders.

That's why a meat-based diet, typically very high in protein (as well as fat, cholesterol, antibiotics, stimulants, bacteria, and pesticide residues) should be avoided by all — and especially by serious athletes.

What's this I hear about vegetarian athletes having more endurance than their meat-eating counterparts?

Yes, it's true. One of the least known benefits of a wholesome vegetarian diet is its energizing effect on stamina and strength.

In the early part of this century, studies at Yale University compared endurance levels of vegetarian and nonvegetarian subjects. Hands down, the vegetarians outlasted and bested the meat eaters in a series of grueling exercises. In fact, vegetarian scores were over double those of nonvegetarians.

And more recently, researchers in Denmark similarly discovered that vegetarian athletes were able to dramatically outperform their meat-eating competitors in various tests of strength and endurance. It appears that the nonvegetarians were literally handicapped by their heavy, meat-based diets. Ironically, instead of making them stronger, flesh foods actually impaired their performance.

In yet another study, this one in France, nonvegetarian participants were found to possess only one-third to one-half the endurance of the vegetarian subjects. What's more, after each exercise, the vegetarians were able to recover their strength in just a fraction of the time that it took the meat eaters to do so.

Why do vegetarians have more stamina and recover quicker than meat eaters?

Athletes need lots of energy to replace the vast amounts used up during strenuous training and competition. And this energy must be supplied by food — but not just any food. The best source of energy is complex carbohydrates, like whole grain breads and pastas, brown rice and other unrefined grains, and beans.

Why are these carbohydrates so great? Because they're digested more quickly and easily than high-fat animal products. In fact, flesh foods seem to use up more energy than they provide — which is why most people feel sluggish and head for the couch after polishing off the roast beef or pork chops. Definitely not the condition for an athlete to be in.

A growing number of experts in the field of sports medicine and nutrition believe that a diet in which three-fourths of all calories come from complex carbohydrates (namely, a varied, wholefoods vegetarian diet) is superior to all others for recharging the body's depleted reservoirs of energy following strenuous physical activity.

And any athlete who can enter a competitive event with a full tank of energy provided by Mother Nature's own specially-blended, high-octane diet will certainly have a tremendous advantage over all the others (unless, of course, there's another vegetarian lurking in the pack!).

Is there any evidence that a vegetarian diet can improve muscle efficiency?

Yes. A recent study by researchers at Oregon State University indicated that long-term vegetarians are endowed with a far greater number of specialized muscle fibers — known as "slow twitch" — than are meat eaters. And these fibers are directly responsible for the way the muscles use oxygen.

In other words, the more slow twitch fibers an athlete has, the greater the stamina and strength will be. It's interesting to note, that these fibers are superabundantly found in such finely-tuned endurance athletes as marathon runners and cyclists.

Perhaps of even greater importance is what these findings could mean for those in the general population — even for those not interested in running 26 miles or cycling across the country. Namely, that the greater the number of slow twitch muscle fibers, the stronger the association with vigorous cardiac health. Which is probably another reason why vegetarians are at such low risk of developing cardiovascular disease.

Why do some vegetarians refuse to feed their pets any meat-based pet foods?

Ethical vegetarians turn thumbs-down on such pet foods because purchasing any meat at all is viewed as supporting the slaughter of animals. Other vegetarians won't buy meat-derived pet foods because of the tremendous waste of resources and damage done to the environment as a result of meat production.

Yet, many others make the decision to keep their dogs or cats away from meat-based pet foods after learning what goes into these products. By law, pet-food manufacturers are allowed to use in their products the meat of diseased and disabled livestock, including cancerous and parasite-infested flesh. In short, pet foods are little more than dumping grounds for the meat industry — where vile, disease-ridden meat-products, totally unfit for human consumption, form the major part of your pet's diet.

But there's something else to be found in each can or bag of pet food — something called, innocently enough, "animal byproducts." They include such unsavory components as arteries, guts, snouts, chicken feet — even hair. To top it off, these so-called nutritious ingredients are loaded with antibiotics, heavy metals, growth hormones, and other toxic residues typically found in slaughtered animals.

It may be surprising to learn that food allergies (especially to meat) are not that uncommon in the pet population. What with all the toxins and chemicals found in meat-based pet foods, it becomes understandable why so many cats and dogs develop food intolerances. Which is another reason why many vegetarians choose to feed their pets a wholesome, meatless diet.

Doesn't it go against their basic nature for dogs and cats to be fed a vegetarian diet?

Not really. After all, does your family pet — that is, "animal companion" — truly resemble the wild, snarling carnivore it may have once been eons ago? Not likely. Dogs and cats aren't wild any longer. They're kept by people and have learned to live a human way of life.

Most pets live indoors, occupy a favorite chair, have their own toys and chewables, and usually sleep on a family member's bed. When it's frigid or damp out, they're reluctant to head out and heed the true call of nature. Many even take walks attired in warm, cozy sweaters. Hardly the way an untamed beast operates.

Many dogs and cats enjoy car rides, take airplane trips, are fed regular meals out of cans or bags, and visit the vet for check-ups and shots. Some are habitually freshened up by professional pet groomers; others are made tidy in the family tub. And when the owners go on vacation, their pets frequently find themselves on a holiday of their own at the kennel.

Is all this in keeping with their wild nature? Of course not. Does all this contravene the laws of nature? Who knows? But one thing's certain. Due to thousands of years of human intervention, your pet has had a total makeover — from savage creature to domestic companion. Therefore, is it really that much more of a violation of your dog's or cat's basic nature to introduce a wholesome, vegetarian diet in place of an unhealthy one? Many people think not.

But how can a vegetarian diet meet the nutritional needs of a carnivorous animal?

While it may be hard to picture a vegetable-eating canine, more and more veterinarians contend that a meatless diet is nutritionally adequate for dogs. And judging by the numerous health problems afflicting many meat-eating dogs — clogged arteries, heart disease, arthritis, and obesity, to mention a few — a vegetarian diet may not only be okay, it may also be the ideal way to go, actually.

In *Dr. Pitcairn's Complete Guide To Natural Health For Dogs and Cats* (see Resources), author and veterinarian Richard Pitcairn refers to a major study in which dogs fed a soy-based diet were found to be in perfect health. Further supporting these claims are the anecdotal accounts of thousands of pet owners whose animals have been thriving for years on vegetarian diets.

However, it's very important for those with animal companions to understand at least the basics of pet nutrition. It shouldn't be too difficult, though, because there are several outstanding books available that are packed with helpful nutritional information, product testimonials, and recipes for making your own pet foods. Besides Dr. Pitcairn's book, these include *Dogs and Cats Go Vegetarian* by Barbara Peden, and *Vegetarian Cats and Dogs* by James Peden (see Resources).

I've read that cats, unlike dogs, just can't be fed a vegetarian diet. Is that so?

It's true that cats are more of a problem than dogs when it comes to a meatless diet. But that's not because felines are too fussy to make the big switch. Rather, cats need certain nutrients that are available only in meat — nutrients that dogs are able to self-produce. Specifically, cats require a usable form of vitamin A and the amino acid taurine. Without them, cats can suffer horrible, disabling ailments.

That's why many pet experts have long been opposed to putting cats on vegetarian diets. However, as research continues in this area, attitudes seem to be changing. A number of nutrition-oriented veterinarians point out that as long as your cat's nutritional needs are met, a vegetarian diet would be perfectly fine.

But what about meat-derived vitamin A and taurine? These indispensable nutrients are now synthetically produced from non-meat sources. Several pet food companies (see Networking) make nutritionally-complete, vegetarian cat foods which contain all the necessary nutrients that cats need to be healthy. These companies also market supplements (made up of vegetarian vitamin A and taurine) which can be added to homemade cat foods in order to make them nutritionally-balanced meals.

Yes, it does take a lot more diligence to properly feed your cat than your dog. But many veterinarians (and cat owners, too) are convinced that a well-planned, wholesome vegetarian diet, one that includes the proper supplementation, can make any cat hale and hearty.

Chapter 5
Lifestyle Issues

How should I handle a dinner invitation from new friends who don't know that I'm a vegetarian?

It's usually best to be upfront about being a vegetarian — and to do so as far in advance of the social occasion as possible. If this disclosure policy makes you a bit queasy, just imagine how you'll feel when your host hands you a dinner plate full of veal scallopini or chicken tetrazzini — made in your honor.

Be sure to explain clearly what you do eat and what you don't. Many meat-eaters are unaware that vegetarians eat no flesh whatsoever — no meat or chicken or fish. Let your host know this. But don't expect him or her to spend all day in the kitchen preparing a meatless meal for you. To be fair, though, your host should see to it that there are things for you to eat — like salads, cooked grains, vegetables, and maybe pasta, too.

If the dinner is very informal, you could help your host by suggesting some easily-prepared, familiar meatless dish — a casserole or stir fry, for example. Even better, volunteer to bring a special vegetarian entree for all to share. On the other hand, if you've been invited to a large, elegant affair, it might be best to proceed in another manner.

What's that?

It shouldn't be difficult to follow the dictates of your vegetarian lifestyle when invited to a large or formal dinner. And it might be easiest in that situation to do so with the least amount of fuss, too. So by not revealing your vegetarianism in advance, you'll give your host the freedom from feeling obligated to prepare a special meal for you — in short, one less headache for the both of you.

Of course, soon after you arrive, it would be considerate to let your host know that since you're a vegetarian you won't be supping on the roast or ribs. Some vegetarians, however, prefer using a little "white lie" to avoid any possibility of controversy. What fib? They say that they're on a rigid medical diet which prohibits animal products. This dodge gives them an excuse for inquiring into the contents of each and every food that's served. (But this sort of inquisition may well be more offensive than enlightening.)

What to eat? Focus on such safe foodstuffs as vegetables, salads, breads, and any meatless side dishes that may grace the table. (Incidentally, having a snack or light meal before the dinner might be a good idea.) Definitely try to find out if meat lurks in any questionable food item, but remember to do so in a low-key manner — no need to make a major sound and light show out of it.

If you're offered a meat dish, just decline as politely as you can. It's okay to say that you're a vegetarian, and leave it at that. By all means resist the temptation to inform the gathering of the horrors of factory farming or about all the fat, cholesterol, antibiotics, hormones, and other toxins found in each piece of meat.

If you learn ahead of time that there won't be a meatless thing to eat, you should ask your host in advance for the liberty to bring individual portions of food for yourself. It that's a problem, skip the dinner; but ask if you can drop over later for the post-supper espresso and gaiety.

What should a vegetarian serve a bunch of carnivorous dinner guests?

Definitely feed them something that's nourishing, scrumptious — and meatless. Don't worry about appearing rude on this last point. Most etiquette experts agree that a vegetarian host has no obligation to serve meat, fish, or fowl to nonvegetarian guests. But that doesn't mean you should hand out plates loaded down with such basic fare as boiled tofu, brown rice, and steamed vegetables. Nor would it be a good idea (unless these carnivores are experienced vegetarian food eaters) to try out radical, exotic, or elaborate meatless dishes.

Instead, why not prepare meals that your guests are already familiar with — minus the meat, of course. A few things that meat eaters easily recognize as "real food" are pasta, lasagna, salads, garlic bread, chili, and lots of other savory dishes that have had the meat left out.

How about whipping up some simple ethnic foods? There are cookbooks galore that feature meatless Indian, Mexican, Asian, and other "foreign" dishes. These meals are wonderful combinations of distinctive flavors, aromas, textures, and colors. There's enough going on in these foods to excite all the senses — so much so that the absence of meat will hardly be noticed.

If cooking really isn't your thing, consider stocking up on the commercially-made vegetarian foods that are found in most health food stores. Many of these use meat-substitutes that look, smell, and even taste like meat dishes. And regardless of whether you do the cooking or buy the foods ready-made, your guests will be delighted to discover just how mouth-watering vegetarian foods can be.

Do vegetarians run into any problems on the job concerning their diet?

It isn't easy being a vegetarian in the workplace; especially when you realize that a significant amount of business is conducted over food — at restaurants, luncheons, business banquets, conventions, company cafeterias, and lunchrooms all over America.

In spite of the fact that many people are beginning to see the connection between meat-eating and a host of serious diseases, flesh foods still seem the popular choice (and often the only menu option) at business meals. For vegetarians, finding something decent to eat can be quite a challenge.

Some vegetarians choose to avoid eating out as much as possible; they simply bring their own nutritious meatless foods from home and eat at their desks. And when it's necessary to wine and dine a client, they choose a restaurant that offers both meat and meatless dishes.

If invited to lunch by a client or co-worker, a vegetarian can easily call the restaurant in advance to check the menu. If no meatless entrees are available, it's not uncommon for an eating establishment to be willing to prepare a special meal for the vegetarian. If that doesn't work, there's usually enough meatless side dishes on the menu, such as salads, breads, steamed vegetables, fruit platters, baked potatoes, etc., to put together a satisfactory meal.

When planning to attend a meeting or convention at a hotel, a vegetarian can usually arrange to have vegetarian meals prepared by simply contacting the hotel caterer as far in advance as possible. Of course, it wouldn't hurt to clarify that a meatless diet includes no flesh foods whatsoever — which will hopefully alert the staff to the fact that vegetarians also stay away from such "meatless" fare as chicken and fish.

What's it like for a vegetarian to be married to a meat eater?

That all depends. If both vegetarian and carnivorous spouses are willing to give and take, to accept and respect each other's differences, to be flexible, and to try and keep a sense of humor — such a "mixed-marriage" can work reasonably well.

The usual situation, as the surveys point out, is where one of the spouses (more often the woman) adopts a vegetarian diet during the marriage. Since most husbands shrink from grocery shopping and cooking, the burden of meal preparation falls on the vegetarian wife. And compromises are a must if the marriage is to continue. With a vegetarian chef in the kitchen, it's not uncommon for the carnivorous spouse to drastically reduce — or even discontinue — meat consumption in the home, but continue eating meat at restaurants, at work, and at other people's homes.

In addition to being open-minded, spouses in successful mixed-marriages stand up for one another when either is under attack because of their dietary choices. Thus, for example, if the vegetarian's in-laws were to be hypercritical, the carnivore would openly support his or her spouse. And vice versa, too.

It's not unusual for the vegetarian spouse to try to convert the carnivore to a meatless diet. A common ploy is to introduce familiar, great-tasting vegetarian dishes, while still cooking minimal amounts of meat; then slowly phasing out the meat. Leaving vegetarian books and pamphlets throughout the house is another way vegetarians attempt to get the message across to their partners.

Is there an ideal way to arrange meals when one spouse wants to eat meat, but the other doesn't?

In some "mixed-marriages" the cook actually prepares separate meals every day — one with meat, the other without. But, as you can imagine, this must get quite tedious day-in-day-out. It could well be a continuing source of tension that nobody needs. Happily, there is a way that a married couple can share their meals — in spite of their dissimilar diets. How's that possible? With a little creative planning, that's how. For example, whip up a Chinese stir-fry with brown rice. At the last moment, add the cooked meat to the carnivore's portion; and tofu to the vegetarian's.

Another meal could feature burgers, fries, and steamed vegetables. Pull out a couple pre-made bean-burgers from the freezer and fry them alongside regular hamburgers (in separate pans, of course). Then slip into whole wheat buns, and voilà — you've got nearly identical meals for carnivore and vegetarian.

Or how about chicken, baked potato, and salad for the meat eater; with tempeh, baked potato, and salad for the plant eater? Care for Mexican food? Pass out the whole-grain tortillas, then dig right into separate bowls filled with a variety of chopped vegetables, cheeses, seasoned tofu, and meats. The carnivore can build a mound of ingredients nearly indistinguishable from the one eaten by the vegetarian — except for the meat on one, and the tofu or cheeses on the other.

What about calling a pizza parlor and ordering one to go? One half can be jam-packed with savory vegetable toppings, the other can have pepperoni or anchovies. Although some vegetarians may find it very difficult to see meat on the table, most others will recognize this as a compromise that enables both husband and wife, carnivore and vegetarian, to dine and be together.

Don't young vegetarians have a harder time than adults coping in a meat-eating world?

Whatever one's age, it's never easy being different. And make no mistake about it — vegetarians are different. However, adult vegetarians do seem to have it easier. After all, it's hard to imagine a co-worker or client surveying your lunch and screaming at the top of his lungs: "Yuck. What's that? It looks weird!"

Unlike grown-ups, young vegetarians have to deal with peer-pressure as they meander through such dietary minefields as school cafeterias, parties, camps, holiday and family gatherings, and eating out. Nevertheless, parents can do many things to help their vegetarian youngsters deal with the stresses of being different. When children are capable of understanding, they should be told why they're vegetarian and what to do when people offer them meat. Some kids boldly proclaim: "I don't eat things that had a face." Others simply say, "my parents feel it's better for me not to eat any meat."

Meeting with the teacher at school to explain your child's vegetarianism and any other dietary "peculiarities" can help avert many an awkward predicament. Some parents even drop off wholesome, commercial treats (packaged, bottled, or canned) with the teacher so their vegetarian children will have something to eat during the many parties and special occasions in the classroom.

Youngsters will be subjected to far less flak from their peers when what comes out of their lunch box doesn't look bizarre. Sandwiches can easily be made to look like "normal" food. Parents can select from a number of whole grain breads that are light in color and which closely resemble white bread. As for the fillings, cheese, and peanut butter and jelly are beyond reproach. Practically everybody eats that. Also, health food stores boast a range of meat-substitutes that look, smell, and taste like real meat.

Another lunch option is a hearty, vegetarian soup or stew that can be eaten right out of the thermos — and out of sight of any young carnivorous critics.

Finally, by joining a local vegetarian organization (or starting one if there isn't any) vegetarians can enjoy the support and friendship of others who follow a similar lifestyle. And young vegetarians will be pleased to know that they're not the only vegetarian kids in the world.

I'm a vegetarian in high school. Can I refuse to dissect animals?

You certainly can. The first thing to do is find out whether your state has a students' rights bill (several states do) which gives all students the right to refuse to dissect. Call your city or county library reference department to find out.

If your state is without such a bill, you should approach your teacher and explain that dissection violates your moral and ethical beliefs. Ask for an alternative assignment that's in keeping with your beliefs. Usually, that's all it takes.

However, you may be told by the teacher that a refusal to dissect will result in a failing grade. Then it's time to take action. Have a parent or other adult take your case to the school district science coordinator — or perhaps the district superintendent. It's even possible that your activism could result in a district policy permitting all students to refuse dissection and pursue non-animal assignments instead.

But what do you do if that fails? A couple of things. You can contact such national organizations as People For the Ethical Treatment of Animals, the National Anti-Vivisection Society, the American Anti-Vivisection Society, or the Animal Legal Defense Fund (see Networking) for advice. You may also be able to interest the American Civil Liberties Union in taking the school district to court. But don't fret over such a tactic. Because long before your case would ever come to trial, the district would likely seek a settlement. Translation: You wouldn't be required to dissect animals.

And why not go even one step further? Consider initiating action that would get a students' rights bill passed by your state legislature. Call your state representative for information on how to go about doing that.

I'm planning a trip abroad. Will it be hard finding vegetarian meals?

That seems to vary from country to country. Vegetarian travellers do report the most positive experiences in India, Italy — and particularly Great Britain, where a strong vegetarian tradition has existed for nearly 150 years. Surprisingly, France, the land of haute cuisine, is not as food-friendly toward vegetarians as you'd think. To a large extent, that's because the typical French cook relies heavily on meat, chicken, and fish for most dishes.

A word now about Asian restaurants. Vegetarians headed to such places as China, Cambodia, Laos, Vietnam, or Thailand need to be aware that Asian cooks routinely use flesh foods, albeit minuscule amounts, as a seasoning, condiment, or ingredient in virtually every traditional dish. You'll likely encounter the same thing in Asian restaurants outside Asia, as well.

However, by doing a little research on the cuisine of the places to be visited, a vegetarian should be able to ferret out the "safe" dishes that can be eaten. Also, it would be very helpful to learn enough of the local language to be able to explain the meaning of the term "vegetarian" — and specifically which foods you will eat, and which you won't.

Many vegetarian voyagers avoid restaurants entirely, instead shopping at sidewalk markets and grocery stores for such meatless staples as fruits, vegetables, breads, cheeses, and prepared beans — and then picnicking in parks, at beaches, and in their hotel rooms. Some adventurers even bring along a small rice cooker or electric fry pan to prepare their locally purchased grains, tofu, and other foodstuffs.

Finally, you may want to order a handbook from the Vegetarian Society of the United Kingdom (Parkdale and Dunhan Road, Altrincham, Cheshire WA14 4QG, United Kingdom) which features organizations, restaurants, and lodging facilities around the world that provide vegetarian meals and services. And by writing ahead to local vegetarian societies, you'll get the scoop on how to maximize the enjoyment of your vegetarian holiday.

Isn't it a hassle getting vegetarian meals on airplanes? •

Not really. Due to the fact that the number of requests for vegetarian meals has skyrocketed in recent years, most airlines have attempted to add tasty, appealing vegetarian foods to their menu offerings.

I say "attempted" because the results can vary from airline to airline (and even from flight to flight). Occasionally the food's first-rate; at times it's dreadful. And every so often, the food is nowhere to be found. Veteran vegetarian travellers suggest that a number of things can be done to insure the delivery of meatless meals to you.

When you make your flight reservations, inform the travel agent or airline representative that you want vegetarian meals. This is the time to mention dairy products and eggs if you want meals without them. After the reservation has been put in the computer, ask the agent or rep to read back your travel arrangements — and make sure that your vegetarian meal request has been noted.

A few days before your departure, call the airline to make certain that your special meal request is still in the computer. There's still time (they need a day) for the airline to reorder the vegetarian meals if your initial request somehow disappeared.

Upon arrival at the airport for your flight check-in, again ask for confirmation of your vegetarian meals.

Unfortunately, if there's no record of your request at that time the airline will have to improvise — and fast. Ask about your options (there's always fruit plates). Even if all's well so far, be sure to inform the flight attendants as you board the plane that you ordered the vegetarian meals.

And when the airborne beverage service begins, it wouldn't hurt to remind the attendants one more time that you're the one (among dozens, no doubt) who requested vegetarian food. If all goes well, you should receive a delicious, vegetarian dish that will look much better than the non-vegetarian meals around you. So much so, that you'll be the envy of your row.

And you should be pleased about that — as well as for another thing. Namely, about not having to dig into your carry-on bag under your seat for the vegetarian food you brought along as "insurance" in case the airline had lost your special food order or given it to another passenger by mistake.

How do vegetarians go about getting meatless meals while hospitalized?

Fortunately, more and more hospitals are recognizing the special dietary needs of their vegetarian patients. Some of the larger facilities even offer vegetarian meals on a regular basis; while many others provide meatless meals, too, although only upon request. But what does a vegetarian do who's hospitalized at an institution that has no tradition of offering vegetarian meals? At these facilities, where the staff typically has had no training in nutrition, vegetarian patients may even be pressured into eating flesh foods.

There are several steps a vegetarian can take to be assured of receiving vegetarian food while in the hospital. Perhaps the simplest is to check into a hospital operated by Seventh-Day Adventists — a Christian church that encourages its members to follow a vegetarian diet. By writing the General Conference of Seventh-Day Adventists (12501 Old Columbia Pike, Silver Spring, MD 20904) you can find out the location of the nearest Adventist hospital.

If there are no Adventist hospitals in your area, call local hospitals and inquire about vegetarian meals. Then choose the one which your doctor is affiliated with and ask to be admitted there. Be sure to inform your physician that you are a vegetarian before he or she submits dietary instructions to the hospital staff. If you avoid dairy products and eggs, you should also have that information added to your dietary orders — or you will be struggling endlessly with nurses and dietitians alike.

Upon entering the hospital, politely remind the admitting nurse and the dietitian that your dietary orders specify vegetarian meals exclusively. Inquire whether the facility has a written policy concerning home-cooked foods being brought in. While most hospitals officially frown on this practice (they fear accidental food poisoning), not a few vegetarian patients have been known to have family and friends smuggle in their favorite vegetarian foods.

A final bit of advice: Get a copy of a helpful vegetarian pamphlet called "Hospital Survival Guide" put out by the Vegetarian Resource Group (see Networking). This little guide is full of valuable tips which should insure that you'll eat well — and vegetarian — while in the hospital.

Chapter 6

Marketing Meat

If vegetarianism is so healthful,
why doesn't the government urge
Americans to follow a low-fat,
meatless diet?

Even the U.S. Government, with all the resources at its
disposal, is unwilling to take on the $60 billion meat
industry, and the millions of factory farmers and ranchers
who raise livestock, and the pharmaceutical industry that
produces all the drugs administered to farm animals, and
the steel industry that supplies the equipment used on
factory farms, and a myriad of other, powerful related
industries.

It's probably safe to say that challenging these conglomerates is about the furthest thing the government
would consider doing, anyway. In fact, its policy is just the
opposite. And the U.S. Department of Agriculture (USDA)
is a perfect example. Here's what I mean. The USDA, as
mandated by Congress, has a dual mission: on one hand,
to safeguard the U.S. food supply; on the other, to actively
promote American agricultural products, including meat,
dairy, and eggs. And it performs this latter function far
more vigorously than it does protecting the American
people. If the USDA warned people to drastically reduce
their consumption of flesh foods, its role as marketer of
agricultural products would be seriously compromised.

Critics boldly assert that the dairy and meat industries actually call the shots at the USDA. But while that

may be an arguable opinion, it is an indisputable fact that the USDA does obtain much of the nutritional information it disseminates — from the meat and dairy industries themselves. And this vitally important information is published in Handbook 8 which is used as the basis for all food-assistance programs in the nation.

Understandably, there aren't many nutrition experts within the government who would dare urge Americans to cut back on their intake of such high-fat foods as meat, poultry, dairy products, and eggs. To do so would invite harsh reactions from the influential meat and dairy associations — reactions which have been known to cut short many a promising career in public service. What's more, each time the U.S. Surgeon General prepares his or her report to the nation, the meat and dairy industries lobby to kill any recommendation for Americans to reduce their consumption of meat.

As a result of such industry influence, most government nutrition reports seem to come out of happy valley — there's no urgency to them, whatsoever. But 500,000 Americans drop dead each year from diet-related heart disease alone. That certainly should be a loud enough wake-up call for the government to break free of the meat and dairy industry grip.

Exactly how do the meat and dairy industries attempt to silence their critics?

In a heavy-handed manner that's all too often reminiscent of the way totalitarian regimes go about stifling free speech and the truth. A few examples should make this perfectly clear.

Several months before author David Steinman's book *Diet For A Poisoned Planet* was to hit the bookstores, lobbying groups set about to make sure that the work would enter this world stillborn. The head of the Environmental Protection Agency was pressured to denounce one of that agency's senior research scientists who had written the introduction to the book.

Pro-industry government officials were urged to condemn both the book and author as threats to the American way of life. A public relations firm was hired to smother the author's publicity tour. As a result of a well-orchestrated campaign, major television and radio talk shows cancelled their planned interviews with Steinman.

After John Robbins' landmark book *Diet For A New America* (which demonstrated the benefits of a vegetarian diet and the harmful effects of meat-eating on the environment) became a popular success, it was time for the industry assault to begin. A national meat-lobbying organization provided a considerable grant to a major Texas university to challenge every assertion in Robbins' book — even to question the author's integrity. All this in order to discredit a book that had touched a nerve across America.

Dairy industry lobbyists went ballistic after a writer dared suggest in a magazine article that cows' milk was really designed for baby cows, not humans. Accordingly, they filed a libel lawsuit against the author and the magazine for their so-called attack on milk's pure image. The legal action was seen as a warning to anyone else who thought of spreading spurious rumors about dairy products.

A public television station in California planned to broadcast a documentary on the dangers of eating meat. However, before the show aired, the station was visited by meat industry representatives — and their lawyer. They warned the station that it could expect a loss of financial support if that particular show were televised. Their intimidation worked; the documentary was put on indefinite hold.

But aren't these just a few isolated cases?

Unfortunately not. They're merely the tip of the iceberg. Perhaps a couple more instances will make it even clearer just how threatened the meat and dairy industries feel by change. In fact, they have much to fear — as more and more Americans are seeing the connection between meat eating, their health, and the environment.

The wrath of cattlemen and pork producers fell like a lightening bolt upon a university biotechnology researcher who insinuated in a radio interview that people should cut back on their intake of red meat. Shortly after the researcher's advice hit the airwaves, the station was flooded with calls from meat industry representatives demanding to know why a state-funded university employee was not supporting the state's important meat industry.

Even the state legislature got into the act. Under pressure to do something, they called the researcher before the senate's Agriculture Committee to determine whether her remarks had done damage to the state's beef and pork industries. Yet another barrage from the legislature took the form of thinly disguised threats to cut funding for the researcher's position — and the university, as well.

Several years ago, superstar country singer k.d. lang participated in a series of television and radio advertisements sponsored by the national animal rights organization, People For the Ethical Treatment of Animals (PETA). These "Meat Stinks" ads were widely broadcast around the country — including the factory farming states.

As feared, reaction was swift and intense from meat industry lobbying groups. Consequently, the singer's records were barred from the airwaves in a number of states; and numerous promoters and concert halls called off her scheduled performances.

With the threat of such industry onslaughts ever looming on the horizon, it's little wonder that many figures in the media, government, and the academic world prefer to keep their "anti-meat bias" to themselves.

If animal products really are damaging to one's health and the environment, why do most Americans continue to eat them?

Because decades of sophisticated advertising campaigns and propaganda have convinced most people that eating meat is healthy and nutritionally sound. In spite of nearly 100 years of scientific evidence linking animal products with illness and environmental destruction, the meat, dairy, and egg industries have successfully concealed the devastating impact of their products.

This crusade to assure Americans that animal products are necessary for their health begins before one is even born. Even obstetricians get into the act by informing pregnant women that meat, milk, and eggs are vital to the well-being of the developing fetus. Later, pediatricians issue this same spurious advice to parents of growing children.

But why are doctors recommending these dangerous eating habits?

Certainly not because they're in league with the meat and dairy industries. On the contrary, most physicians are well-intentioned, hardworking professionals — but they simply don't have the training or time to devote to good nutrition.

Besides, much of the "nutritional education" they receive in medical school is provided by the meat and dairy industries. That's right. Most people don't know that these industries flood medical schools and universities that train dieticians, with educational materials on nutrition — which, of course, emphasize the importance of meat, milk, and eggs in a healthy diet.

Also, these same schools that train America's health professionals, typically use nutrition textbooks that warn students against recommending such "fad diets" as vegetarianism. Not surprisingly, these texts are supported by generous grants from meat industry lobbying groups. There's more. Industry organizations funnel millions of dollars to major teaching universities to conduct friendly studies of the nutritional values and benefits of the donor's products. In these and other ways, the meat, dairy, and egg industries disburse astounding amounts of money to keep doctors, dieticians, and other health professionals thinking positive thoughts about animal products.

Perhaps the most shameful part of the meat and dairy industries' public relations program is the effort directed at children in the classroom.

What do you mean by that?

Children are a special challenge. The slick propaganda campaigns directed at youngsters must overcome their natural affinity and love for living animals. Rising to the challenge, the meat, dairy, and egg industries pull out all the stops to convince children that cows, pigs, and chickens do not suffer. And what more proof is needed than all those laughing, dancing, grinning farm animals seen in commercials, on highway billboards, on packaging — and especially in the so-called educational materials supplied by industry lobbyists to public school classrooms all across America.

From the earliest age, school children are taught the importance of the daily consumption of foods from the basic four food groups — in other words, of consuming lots of meat, milk, cheese, and eggs. Industry promotional materials portray farm animals as happy, contented animals; no mention being made of the brutal realities of factory farming and slaughterhouses.

To rebut those who argue that meat production severely damages the environment, meat industry trade groups sponsor educational campaigns in elementary schools around the country. Pamphlets and leaflets sent to these schools praise the virtues of cattlemen everywhere — all of whom are represented as using only gentle, humane, ecological methods in raising their calves and cows. In fact, the meat industry itself is presented as the true conservationists of America's soil, water, and other valuable resources.

What with all this propaganda — initially aimed at young children — bombarding the public from the meat and other lobbying groups, it's not surprising that most people think that animal products are necessary for good health.

Why don't we hear more about studies like the one that showed how a low-fat, vegetarian diet can reverse heart disease?

Most research dollars flow from special interest groups that have no desire whatsoever to prove the health-promoting and healing effects of a wholesome, vegetarian diet. Nutritional research funds typically come from drug companies and meat, dairy, and egg lobbyists — all with huge research budgets and equally-large intentions of profiting handsomely from research findings. Which is why these groups have never been accused of cozying up to vegetarianism.

After all, a vegetarian diet that's chock full of whole grains, legumes, fruits, and vegetables can't be made into pills and sold for exorbitant prices. Nor does the sale of plant-based foods result in extraordinary profits for any-one — as, on the contrary, does the merchandising of meat, dairy products, and eggs.

And that now-famous study you cite by Dean Ornish, M.D., showing how a vegetarian diet can stop and even reverse cardiovascular disease (without drugs and costly, dangerous bypass surgery!) — almost never took place. All major funding sources refused to finance the study. Eventually, Dr. Ornish found a private sponsor — a health-minded, Texas land developer — and the life-saving research project was rescued from the trash heap.

With considerable meat, dairy, and egg industry funds flowing to friendly universities and research groups to "prove" that animal products promote health, it's under-standable why so many Americans continue to follow a destructive, flesh-foods diet. And without access to unbi-ased nutritional information, most people won't make the dietary changes that could significantly lower their risks of contracting cancer, heart-disease, osteoporosis, and other life-threatening and crippling diseases.

Despite our high-meat diets, aren't we living much longer than Americans did just a century ago?

Well, get ready to see just how easy it is to be fooled by statistics. Although it may be hard to believe, it's an indisputable fact that not only many of those living in the 19th century, but also even a fair number of citizens of ancient Rome actually lived as long or longer than modern Americans.

But how can that be? Isn't it common knowledge that the people of ancient times had life expectancies of only 25 years; and Americans in the 1800's lived just to the ripe old age of 45? So how can it be said that Americans aren't better off today?

People living in the days of the old Roman empire did have average life expectancies of 25 years — but only because of incredibly-high infant mortality rates that drastically lowered the overall population's statistical averages. Here's what I mean. For instance, in a society of 30 people, 10 live to be 75 years old, but 20 die before reaching their first birthday. Statistically, each member's average life expectancy is 25 years (10 x 75 = 750 years plus 20 x 1 = 20 years, for a total of 770 years. Then, divide 770 by 30 people = 25 year average).

As the example shows, however, if a person survived infancy, he or she lived a long life indeed. Another thing is evident: Statistical averages tell you very little about how people really live.

In the past century, modern medicine and other improvements have sharply reduced infant mortality, allowing more people to reach their golden years. But even with all the new drugs and high-tech medical procedures available today, a modern American's life expectancy is merely a few years more than it was in the mid-1800's. In effect, we're not really living that much longer than our ancestors — recent or ancient.

Why aren't we?

Ironically, just when modern medicine and improvements in public sanitation and personal hygiene had dramatically cut infant mortality rates and banished such epidemic killers as influenza, smallpox, typhoid fever, pneumonia, and tuberculosis — Americans traded in their simple, healthy diet for one high in meat, milk, and fat.

In the old days, most people ate wholesome food like whole grains, beans, fruits, vegetables, and just a little meat a few times a week. Nearly a vegetarian diet, in fact! Our ancestors worked hard and ate hearty, natural foods.

But as the 20th century dawned, many factors (not the least of which were the vigorous promotional efforts of the expanding meat and dairy industries) influenced Americans to change the way they ate. Out went a largely plant-based diet; in came one rich in meat, dairy products, and eggs.

As a result, a host of "new" diseases were to afflict Americans from then on: cancer, heart disease, strokes, osteoporosis, diabetes, hypertension, and other diet-related ailments. And a hoped-for, dramatic increase in life expectancy, which should have accompanied the rise in modern medicine, failed to ever materialize. The culprit? A diet heavily laden with high-fat meat and animal products.

And while the meat, dairy, and egg industries want you to believe that Americans are healthier and living much longer than ever before, it just isn't so. As Dean Ornish, M.D., indicates, over 40 million Americans suffer from cardiovascular disease, 60 million have high blood pressure, and 80 million have blood cholesterol levels that are dangerously high. Further, with 10,000 Americans dropping dead each week from heart attacks and strokes alone, many health conscious professionals feel that it's cruel and self-serving for the meat and dairy industries to continue assuring Americans how healthy they are.

But as long as people go along with such a biased

representation, they'll feel no need to radically depart from a meat-based diet. Which, of course, is good news for the industries that make a killing selling animal products.

I read about a study in the newspaper that said cutting back to a "low-fat" diet doesn't reduce cancer risks. Can that be true?

When industry-sponsored half-truths like that appear in the media, it only encourages meat eaters to continue following the high-fat standard American diet which has been unquestionably linked to a host of serious diseases. It also keeps the cash registers abuzz for the meat, dairy, and egg industries.

Currently, Americans are advised by many national health organizations to follow a "low-fat" diet which limits fat intake to no more than 30 percent of total calories. Yet a number of eminent researchers intensely dispute that figure, recommending instead that only 10 to 15 percent of calories come from fat. They argue convincingly that the 30 percent figure is hardly "low-fat"; and that it actually serves the interests of the meat, dairy, and egg industries only too well by encouraging Americans to follow a diet high in animal products.

So how much fat does the average meat eater consume? Brace yourself. Nearly half — that's 50 percent! — of all calories come from fat. And if a diet that's 30 percent fat is considered unnecessarily high in fat and unhealthy — what does that make one that's 50 percent fat? Extremely hazardous to one's health, that's what.

In that misleading study you cite, it was concluded that decreasing dietary fat from 50 percent to about 30 to 35 percent would not reduce the risks of cancer. Of course it shouldn't! Because a diet that's 30 to 35 percent fat is still dangerously unhealthy. So even reducing fat intake, but still remaining at or above 30 percent, does not improve health, at all.

Cynically, the meat, dairy, and egg industries jumped on the deceiving findings and made them a part of their propaganda campaign to convince Americans that cutting back on their intake of animal products would bear no dividends. But this is an especially cruel piece of trickery, one based wholly on economic self-interest, since numerous studies indisputably link a high-fat diet with cancer, heart disease, osteoporosis and other serious life-threatening disorders.

And while a level of 30 percent dietary fat intake is a reasonable, intermediate goal for all those consuming 50 percent fat, many distinguished researchers, among them Dean Ornish, M.D., John McDougall, M.D., and Michael Klaper, M.D., strongly urge adult Americans to reduce their dietary fat intake to no more than 10 to 15 percent of total calories.

CLOG AND BLOCK'S® CORN CHIPS

NUTRITIONAL INFORMATION
PER SERVING

SERVING SIZE · · · · · · · · · · · · · 1 OZ
NUMBER OF SERVINGS IN BAG · · · · 8
CALORIES PER SERVING · · · · · · · 144
PROTEIN · · · · · · · · · · · · · · · · · · 2 GRAMS
CARBOHYDRATES · · · · · · · · · · 16 GRAMS
FAT · 8 GRAMS

How can you tell from looking at a package label what percentage of the calories comes from fat, anyway?

Until every food manufacturer is required to post that information on the label, you'll just have to do the calculating yourself. As it now stands, the typical product label only lists the number of grams of fat in each serving — but how many Americans are familiar with metric units, anyhow? (And doing it this way keeps people from realizing how excessively-fatty most packaged foods are.)

For example, the label above shows that each serving of corn chips contains eight grams of fat. Is that a lot of fat? Does that put the product in the low-fat 10 to 15 percent range, or in the unhealthy 30 percent or more category? You can figure that out — with a little number-crunching, that's all.

Start by knowing that in each gram of fat there are nine calories (as opposed to only four calories in each gram of protein or carbohydrates). Again, looking at the label above, you can see that each serving contains, among other things, 144 calories and eight grams of fat. Armed with these figures, you're now ready to compute the percentage of calories from fat.

Multiplying the fat grams by nine results in 72 fat calories (8 grams x 9 calories = 72). Next, dividing the fat calories (72) by the number of calories in each serving (144) tells you that Clog & Block's corn chips get 50 percent of their calories from fat. Clearly, a high-fat food.

Incidentally, most nutritionists advise that you calculate your fat intake on a daily basis — rather than meal-by-meal. Thus, the choice of a high-fat lunch, for example, can be balanced by eating fat-free or very low-fat meals at breakfast and dinner.

Shouldn't the fast-food chains be praised for developing burgers that are only 10 percent fat?

I wouldn't be too quick to compliment the fast-food industry for their so-called fat-free burgers — especially after you learn of the deception employed to convince the public that a greasy piece of meat is really low in fat. I'll explain.

There are two generally accepted, reliable methods of indicating the fat content of all foods. As previously noted, measuring the percentage of calories derived from fat provides an accurate way of determining whether any particular food is "low-fat" or "high-fat."

The other legitimate method, though not without its

critics, of revealing the fat content of any food, is to indicate how many grams of fat are found in each serving. Obviously then, high-fat foods would show a significantly higher number of fat grams than would low-fat foods. A person wanting to limit his or her intake of fat could then keep track of how many grams of fat were eaten each day.

But these straightforward techniques of measuring fat content strike terror in the hearts of the meat, dairy, and egg industries. Why? Because those methods would reveal that all animal products (and even some non-flesh foods) are dangerously high in fat.

Which brings us now to a terribly misleading way of measuring fat content — one that is used to successfully conceal just how high in fat animal products actually are.

Which way is that?

By weight. The fast-food chains measure the fat content of their high-fat foods as a percentage of their total weight. Here's how this piece of trickery works. A burger patty, for example, checks in with 130 calories and seven grams of fat. By legitimate standards, that burger gets nearly half of its calories from fat (7 grams x 9 calories = 63 fat calories; 63 fat calories ÷ 130 total calories = 49 percent fat).

But watch what the fast-food giants do in order to claim that a 49 percent fat-burger is nothing but a 10 percent fat-burger. First, they add up the total weight of the whole burger patty, the bun, and all the trimmings. Then, they divide the fat (seven grams) by the total weight of the sandwich. By this hocus-pocus, it can now be asserted that a high-fat burger is really a low-fat one.

Here's another way of looking at this deception. Ask the butcher for a hunk of fat. Unquestionably, all the calories from that blob of fat are fat-derived. It's 100 percent pure fat. Let's say you want to go into business selling lumps of fat. But would your customers really want such a high-fat product? If only there were some way to get away with claiming that your chunk of fat was actually low-fat.

And as luck would have it, you discover the fat-by-weight measuring method. With that trick up your sleeve, you decide to go into the soup business. Your recipe couldn't be simpler: just dump a fat blob in a bowl of piping hot water. Although your broth, just like the piece of fat, really gets 100 percent of its calories from fat, you can advertise it as 90 percent fat-free — thanks to the fat-by-weight technique.

You're able to get away with this ruse by dividing the weight of the fat by the total weight of the soup (comprised of fat plus water). By this unscrupulous measuring method, you've magically transformed a 100 percent pure fat product that gets all of its calories from fat, into a bouillon that's touted as being only 10 percent fat. In other words, you've made it 90 percent fat-free. And you did this without removing even a drop of fat.

Most people are confused enough about fat consumption without being tricked into believing that a high-fat slab of meat is really low-fat health food. It's irresponsible and cruel of the meat industry to pitch these burgers to consumers who need to cut down on fat. Because any way you measure it, the fat from those burgers will still clog up your arteries.

By the same token, isn't it deceiving to call "2 percent" milk a low-fat product?

You're absolutely right. It's nothing but the same ploy of measuring fat by weight in order to give the impression that a product is low in fat. And many who want to limit their intake of fat have been led to believe that in 2 percent milk only two percent of its calories are derived from its fat content. But as you'll see, that's simply not the case at all.

A single eight ounce glass of 2 percent milk contains 145 calories and five grams of fat. Since there are nine calories in each gram of fat, you can see that the glass of milk has 45 calories of fat (5 x 9 = 45). And those 45 fat calories represent 31 percent of the total calories of that dairy product (45 ÷ 145 = 31 percent). Hardly low-fat.

Fearing that most Americans might hesitate to regularly drink a beverage that was almost one-third fat, the dairy industry resorted to measuring the fat by weight to make this high-fat content sound enticingly low.

Here's how they do it. An eight ounce glass of 2 percent milk weighs 240 grams. Of those 240 grams, five grams are of fat. After dividing the fat grams by the total weight, you arrive at the 2 percent figure (5 ÷ 240 = 2 percent). And while the fat may only represent 2 percent of the milk's total weight, it also represents a significant 31 percent of the product's calories.

The only milk that comes close to genuinely being called "2 percent" is skim milk — which gets about five percent of its calories from fat.

I've heard about studies that prove eating high cholesterol foods won't raise cholesterol levels. How's that possible?

That's only possible when you design the experiments to yield the results you want — which is exactly what's been done in these studies sponsored by the meat, dairy, and egg industries. After all, doesn't it make perfectly good business sense for industries that sell lots of high profit meat, dairy products, and eggs — all cholesterol-rich foods — to convince people that the animal products they eat do not raise blood cholesterol levels?

But how can you design studies that will defy the laws of nature in order to show that eating lots of cholesterol magically has no boosting effect on the body's own blood cholesterol levels? Easy. Just pick subjects for your studies who already have dangerously high cholesterol levels. Because it's an indisputable fact that once your blood is saturated with cholesterol, there's nothing more you can do to make things worse (as far as cholesterol is concerned).

Back to the rigged studies. Then these cholesterol-saturated subjects are fed high cholesterol foods like beef, eggs, or chicken; and to no one's surprise the subjects' blood cholesterol levels do not rise. Of course they can't rise — they're sky-high already.

So in spite of all the honest impartial studies showing that cholesterol-rich animal products do indeed inflate blood cholesterol levels, the meat, dairy, and egg industries still proceed to issue press releases by the thousands trumpeting the "proof" that their products do not raise cholesterol levels. It's yet another industry triumph; and another sad example of commercial interests winning out over public health.

What other deceptions do the meat, dairy, and egg industries use to cast their products in a positive light?

A common meat industry trick is to calculate cholesterol or fat using unrealistically small serving sizes. For example, an ad touting the health benefits of beef will proclaim that studies have shown that a three ounce serving of steak is very low in cholesterol and fat — while hiding the fact that the average serving of steak weighs in at six ounces or more.

Also, by using scalpels, lab personnel working on those industry-supported studies are able to surgically remove every visible trace of fat from the meat — creating low-fat beef samples that no shopper will ever find in any supermarket. Not surprisingly, after being "analyzed," the beef is pronounced low in fat.

Similarly, a major chicken producer runs nationwide advertisements in all the media smugly calling attention to its consumer-friendly nutrition labels affixed to every package of chicken. Trouble is, while a customary serving of chicken ranges between four and six ounces, the package labels cunningly disclose the fat, cholesterol, and calories for one ounce servings only. Chicken, by all standard measuring practices, is high in both cholesterol and saturated fat — but with a little imaginative reporting, it can strike one as being practically a health food.

Another effective strategy to fool the public uses phony comparisons to better position a product. For instance, a corned beef manufacturer (with a product that's about 55 percent fat) can show that its corned beef is not fatty at all, that is, when compared to a wide range of familiar foods like cream cheese, cream, butter, olives, salad dressing, mayonnaise, coconut, and so forth. What's not revealed in the comparison is the fact that, except for the beef, all those foods are each around 90 to 100 percent fat. Of course, corned beef should smell like a rose in comparison.

And probably the best way for a company to show that its meat or dairy products aren't really that high in cholesterol is to contrast them with eggs — the most cholesterol-saturated food on the planet. Except, they usually don't indicate that last point in the comparisons.

How can you be on the alert for other misleading studies and claims?

There are several things that discriminating readers can do to protect themselves from biased reporting. From the start, always keep in mind that most of the funding for nutritional research comes from the meat, dairy, egg, and pharmaceutical industries — powerful groups with keen financial interests in proving that their products are healthful and necessary.

When you hear of a scientific discovery, try to find out where the money for that research came from: was it from food and drug industries or from a government agency or public interest group? Ask yourself who will benefit economically from the study results.

Be wary of dated studies used as "proof." When a lobbying group cites a study to support its claim, inquire about the status of that study. Is it current? If it's an early study, the findings may well have been invalidated by more recent research.

Focus on certain particulars. How many people were analyzed in the study? A small sampling may not be very useful in drawing conclusions applicable to the general public. Generally, the fewer the subjects, the less credible the study.

Did the study focus on authentic situations and populations — from which valid, real-life conclusions can be drawn; or was most of the research carried out in labs under simulated conditions?

What about the groups examined in the study? It's not uncommon for industry-supported researchers to compare sickly vegetarians on junk food diets (if they can find them) with relatively disease-free meat-eaters. Such highly questionable methods typically lead to the false notion that meat eating is healthful, while a vegetarian diet is not.

Also, be aware that many nutrition writers in the

media may have little personal experience in the areas they write about. And much of their information may come from publications and other sources supplied by the major food and drug industry lobbying organizations.

You don't need a degree in nutrition to keep from being fooled by industry studies — merely a vigilant eye, a healthy skepticism of self-serving claims, and an open mind for the wholesome alternatives to the standard American meat-based diet.

Appendix I
Glossary

Almond Milk

For those wishing to avoid cow's milk, almond milk makes an excellent substitute and can be used in any recipe that calls for milk. Try it on cereal, as a drink, and in breads, cookies, pancakes, desserts and many other dishes.

Almond milk, available in most natural foods stores, comes packaged in quart-size, aseptic containers that give it a long shelf-life. But if you have a little time, why not make it yourself — it's a snap. All you need are almonds, water, and a blender.

Here's how to do it. Take two cups of shelled almonds, rinse several times, then soak overnight in water. The next day, blend each one-half cup of almonds with two cups of cold water in a blender for a minute until smooth. Then strain the creamy white almond milk through a fine mesh sieve (or cheesecloth) to separate the pulp from the milk.

If you prefer, you can flavor the almond milk with a tad of any natural sweetener, vanilla, and salt. And blending a banana or other fresh fruit with flavored almond milk makes a tasty, nutritious "milkshake." Incidentally, you can make "milk" in the same manner using other nuts and seeds like pecans, walnuts, cashews, and sunflower seeds.

Beans

As more and more health-conscious and economy-minded Americans are discovering — beans can be a delightful source of high-quality protein, vitamins, and minerals, as well as complex carbohydrates and fiber. And being very low in fat, beans make an ideal substitute for meat . To boot, they're a snap to prepare and can be used in a myriad of colorful, aromatic, and flavorful dishes.

To find the widest variety of beans just pop into any natural foods store. You'll find such beans (usually sold in bulk) as lima, kidney, soy, mung, black, navy, fava, great northern, azuki, garbanzo, pinto, and lentils. Later on, we'll take a closer look at some of these.

But first, let's cover some bean basics. After you've selected your beans, it'll be necessary to sort through them and discard any discolored, cracked, or shrivelled beans (the taste and quality of these are not good). And since most bean producers don't really pick through their beans, you'll have to sort out any stones, twigs, or other foreign matter you may find in your bean pile. It's probably easiest just to spread out your beans on a cookie sheet and dig in.

After you've picked over your beans, be sure to rinse them very well. Before cooking, the beans should be soaked for six to eight hours — or better yet, overnight. It's not a bad idea to refrigerate the beans while soaking to prevent them from fermenting. (Soak the beans by pouring them into a bowl and adding at least three times their volume of water.) Soaking not only softens the beans and cuts down on the amount of cooking time, it also helps break down and remove the indigestible bean starches that can cause flatulence.

An alternative soaking process is the "quick-soak." Some studies claim that this technique is even more effective at minimizing flatulence than the overnight soaking method. Do the quick-soak by pouring the beans into a pot and adding several times their volume of water. Bring the water to a boil, then turn off the heat and let the beans soak for at least an hour before cooking.

Incidentally, there are several products on the market that are reported to be successful at minimizing the intestinal discomfort some people experience from eating beans. One of these is called Beano, another is BeSure. These products are enzymes (in liquid or capsules) that are consumed along with the beans to help break down any indigestible starches that make it past the soaking process.

Regardless of your soaking method, before cooking be sure to discard the soaking water since it's loaded with gas-forming starches liberated from the beans. Drain and rinse the beans, then place them in the cooking pot. Cover with water, bring to a boil, then lower the heat and simmer until the beans are soft and delicate (when done they should mash easily between your fingers). While cooking, the beans should not be tightly covered, instead leave the lid ajar — this keeps the cauldron from foaming over. During the cooking process, the beans need to be covered with water. If you find it necessary to add more water during the cooking process to keep the beans covered be sure it's boiling water you're adding (cold water will lengthen cooking time).

The time to add your seasonings is after the beans are cooked. If, for example, you add salt early on, you'll just make the beans tougher, requiring longer cooking time. Cooked beans do well for up to a week under refrigeration or for several months if frozen. Which is why it's a great idea to cook up your beans in batches that exceed your immediate needs and then store the rest for another time when you need a quick, easy-to-prepare meal.

Dry (uncooked) beans, by the way, can be stored for at least a year if kept in a dry, cool place in airtight containers. However, it's best to use up your beans within a few months of their purchase as they lose quality the longer they're stored.

In general, one cup of dry beans is cooked with four cups of water to yield 2½ cups of cooked beans — enough to feed four people. There are many fine vegetarian cookbooks on the market (see Appendix III) that extol the virtues of bean cookery. Look into any of these books and you'll be amazed at all the delightful recipes that call for the humble bean.

There are a few more things to keep in mind as you start to add beans to your diet. The smaller beans (i.e. azuki and lentils) tend to be more digestible than the larger kinds (i.e. kidney beans). Also, you can further help yourself avoid flatulence by eating small portions of beans at first. A maximum of one-half cup cooked beans at a time should help break in your digestive system slowly.

Interestingly, the more often you eat beans the less gas problems you'll have. It seems that most people who get intestinal distress from beans are those who eat them infrequently. Finally, if you haven't a moment to spare to cook beans why not pick up a jar or can of precooked organic beans from the natural foods store. It's a convenient way for you to add a high-quality, nutritious food to your diet — even if you are pinched for time.

A few of my favorite beans include:

• **Azuki Beans:** These small red beans make a good choice for those new to bean cookery. That's because azuki — also called adzuki or aduki — beans are considered to be among the most digestible and fastest cooking of all beans. They don't need to be presoaked before cooking and can even be cooked with rice or other grains in the same pot.

Cooked azuki beans can also be added to any separately-cooked grain dish, tossed into cold salads, and mixed into soups and stews. If you run out of pinto beans for a recipe, just try substituting azuki beans. They taste very similar, although azuki are more delicate. One cup of azuki beans with four cups of water will yield about two cups of cooked beans after cooking for 45 minutes (or until tender).

• **Garbanzo Beans:** Even many people who shy away from beans will make an exception for these slightly crunchy, nutty-flavored, golden beans. Also known as chickpeas — although they don't look like peas — garbanzo beans are the heart and soul of such popular Middle Eastern foods as hummus (a dip made of mashed garbanzos, sesame oil or sesame seed butter, and seasonings) and felafel (ground up garbanzos formed into croquettes).

There are so many culinary things to do with garbanzo beans that entire books have been written on the subject. Cold garbanzo beans make a wonderful addition to any salad — be it pasta, grain, or green. Hot chickpeas are great combined with steaming fluffy grains, and in casseroles, stews, and soups.

Garbanzo beans are quite hard and need to be soaked overnight (or quick-soaked) prior to cooking. One cup of garbanzos cooked with four cups of water for one hour will produce about two cups of cooked beans.

• **Lentils:** Although lentils come in lots of colors, generally only the brown (sometimes called "green") and red varieties are available in the U.S. These small, disk-shaped legumes are an ideal "fast" food — they don't have to be soaked before cooking and in only a half-hour brown lentils cook to a creamy, smooth texture and an earthy, almost peppery flavor. Red lentils cook even faster than that and are milder than browns. Also, since red lentils are very small and thin, they turn to a mushy texture after cooking — making them perfect for puréeing and adding to soups.

But lentils should be thought of for more than just soup. Try making delicious lentil loaves, burgers, casseroles, and dips. Lentils also go well in salads, curried stews, combined with noodles and whole grains, and sautéed with onions, garlic, and bell peppers.

Here's something else about lentils — they're incredibly easy to digest and not very likely to cause flatulence. Cook one cup of lentils with four cups of water; in about 30 minutes you'll have two cups of cooked lentils.

Carob Powder

Carob powder is just the thing for chocolate lovers who wish to avoid the skin problems, intestinal upsets, caffeine, and allergic reactions that can result from eating chocolate. Made from the dried pods of a Mediterranean tree, carob powder looks, feels, and tastes a lot like cocoa powder, except it's low in fat and free of caffeine.

In addition, carob powder is naturally rich in fiber and calcium. It can be substituted for cocoa powder when making sweets and beverages. Try combining carob powder, honey (or maple syrup), peanut butter, salt, and vanilla (experiment with the quantities to suit your taste).

Stir until smooth. This "sauce" will make a great topping on cupcakes, cookies, non-dairy ice creams — or just eat it straight from the bowl.

Coffee Substitutes

Aware of the ill effects of caffeine (nervousness, headaches, faster heartbeat, etc.) many coffee drinkers might be pleased to know that healthful alternatives exist. Several companies make powders and "crystals" that instantly dissolve in hot water to create a rich, coffee-like beverage — but without any caffeine.

Well-known brands of coffee substitutes include Roma, Postum, Cafix, Pero, and Inka. These products are primarily made from roasted grains, roots, and seeds that have been ground into fine black or brown particles. Try several brands to find the one that tastes most like coffee. Of course, fanatical coffee drinkers may need a little time to develop an appreciation for this new brew. It has a unique, pleasant flavor — but it isn't coffee. Then again, it's caffeine-free, also.

I've found that the stronger the cup of grain coffee, the better the taste. To get this, simply try doubling the amount called for on the label. Thus, if one teaspoon per cup is suggested, use two. The brew will be richer, darker, and more like coffee.

Egg Replacer

Eggs can be completely eliminated from baked goods by using granulated egg replacers found at most natural foods stores. Egg replacers are essentially a mixture of starches and leavening agents that act like eggs to lighten (or leaven) and bind the ingredients together.

One of these products, called Ener-G Egg Replacer, contains no eggs, chemical additives, or other animal products. Although it's a powder, Ener-G can be used just like eggs in breads, cakes, cookies, muffins, pancakes, crepes, and so forth. It can also be whipped and used in nonbaked recipes that call for egg whites, such as meringues. A few other uses include mayonnaise and quiches. For each egg you want to replace, just use one teaspoon egg replacer plus two tablespoons of water.

However, you won't be able to use egg replacers in recipes where eggs comprise the chief ingredient. So don't even try to fix a dish of scrambled eggs using egg replacers. It simply won't work. Another thing. Some brands of commercial egg replacers may contain egg whites, dairy products, and chemical additives. Be sure to check the package label if you wish to avoid them.

Frozen Desserts (dairy-free)

Giving up dairy products doesn't have to mean missing out on rich and creamy frozen desserts. With soy-based products becoming ever more popular with the public, natural foods manufacturers are creating great-tasting frozen "ice cream" products in a number of exotic flavors (plus vanilla and chocolate, of course). Also, these dairy-free delights are available in pint and quart sizes, and as ice cream cookies, sandwiches, and dipped-bars.

What's more, these cool, ambrosian treats usually have much less fat and fewer calories than their frozen dairy counterparts. They're also cholesterol-free. And many use organic ingredients and shy away from artificial additives and stabilizers.

Two of the best-known brands include Ice Bean, a soy milk product, and Rice Dream which uses sweet, fermented rice instead of soy. Caution: These products are liable to make you forget all about ice cream.

Meat Analogs

Also known as fake meats, meat analogs are meat look-and-taste-alikes. They're typically made from soy beans and/or grains (sometimes with seeds and nuts, too) plus oil and seasonings and then shaped into familiar meat products. Peer into any natural foods store freezer case or refrigerator and you'll see **meatless** hot dogs, hamburgers, "chicken" nuggets, cold cuts, bologna, steak, "fish" sticks, TV dinners and plenty others.

While these meat analogs may not come across exactly like the "real" things, many of them — especially when prepared or served with familiar condiments or seasonings — come awfully close (which both pleases some vegetarians, and revolts others). Whatever the propriety of vegetarians eating mock meats, meat analogs can satisfy cravings for real meat without animals having to be killed or the environment being harmed or one's health being endangered.

And as far as health goes, fake meats usually have less calories and fat than real meat, and none of the cholesterol or harmful toxins that are usually found in flesh foods.

Meat analogs can be especially helpful for those in need of a quick, easy-to-fix meal, for carnivores in transition to vegetarianism, for vegetarians and meat eaters who want to add a healthful alternative to their regular menus, and even for keeping vegetarian youngsters meatless. Being able to prepare meatless versions of popular dishes can help all vegetarians — particularly young people — feel less different than their peers.

Meatless franks and burgers are ideal for cookouts and birthday parties; and vegetarian cold cuts make great tasting (and looking) sandwiches in any child's lunchbox. Many brands of fake meats are so meatlike that most kids don't even know that they're eating plant foods.

However, since some brands are definitely better than others, it's not a bad idea to experiment between them to find the products that come closest to matching the tastes and textures that you're looking for. And don't forget to read labels in order to find the vegetarian meats lowest in fat and sodium.

Miso

Miso (pronounced me-so) is a thick, spreadable fermented paste made from soybeans, grains, and salt. It's used for flavoring in sauces, soups, salad dressings, gravies, dips, spreads, and numerous other dishes. This traditional Japanese food comes in a myriad of colors, aromas, and flavors. Generally, the light-colored misos are milder and sweeter than the darker varieties, which tend to be saltier and stronger-flavored.

Since miso is a fermented food, it contains valuable enzymes and beneficial bacteria which both aid in digestion and impart key nutrients. As such, miso should not be boiled — which would kill the microorganisms and de-activate the enzymes. Instead, stir miso into a dish at the end of the cooking process. Or, if adding miso to soups, first dissolve the miso in a little water. Then add to the simmering soup, and serve. In this way, miso's healthful properties can come to you with minimal loss.

Experiment with light and dark misos in many dishes to find your favorite combinations. If you have the choice, select unpasteurized misos, as they are better tasting and more nourishing than pasteurized ones. You should store miso tightly covered and under refrigeration. It'll last for months that way.

Keep in mind that miso imparts a wonderfully complex taste to any dish — and a little goes a long way. That's especially important to keep in mind since miso is rela-tively high in salt. And for those wishing to learn more about this tasty, versatile, nutritious food, I highly suggest *The Book of Miso* by William Shurtleff and Akiko Aoyagi (Ballantine Books, 1988).

Nutritional Yeast

Sometimes referred to as **brewer's yeast**, nutritional yeast is a highly-nourishing, tasty food product that can double as a condiment and a food supplement. Rich in B-complex vitamins and trace minerals (also high in protein and low in calories) nutritional yeast adds a cheesy or nutty (some even say "meaty") flavor to any dish it's added to.

Nutritional yeast is usually found as yellow powder or flakes. Add it to soups, gravies, stir fries, casseroles, dips, and many other dishes. Some people think it tastes like Parmesan cheese and use brewer's yeast as they would that dairy product. A sprinkling on popcorn imparts a cheesy flavor and makes a healthy salt substitute for those watching their sodium intakes.

Be sure to sample the various brands to find which tastes best. Some brands can be strong, others are quite savory. Also, by checking the package or bulk container labels, you can compare the nutritional make-up (i.e. as to B vitamins, minerals, and trace elements) of each brand of yeast.

Seitan

Also called **kofu**, or **wheat meat**, seitan (pronounced say-tan) is a nourishing, easily-digestible, low-fat, low-calorie food made from wheat. It's quite high in protein (about 15 grams in each 4-ounce serving), supplies a modest amount of vitamins and minerals, and is completely free of cholesterol.

Most natural foods stores carry seitan in small plastic tubs under refrigeration. As with tofu, there's an expiration date which should be checked to insure getting the freshest product.

Seitan, a chewy, meatlike, hearty-flavored product, makes a wonderful meat-substitute in many dishes. It can be added to pasta salads, stir-fried vegetables, casseroles, and stews. Seitan can also be served as cutlets, between slices of whole wheat bread, or in lasagnas. It's even firm enough to be basted and grilled.

Seitan can even be made at home. It's fresher, cheaper, and tastier to make your own — and not difficult at all. Here's how. Start off with seven cups of whole wheat flour (not pastry flour since that doesn't have enough gluten to make seitan) and three cups of water. Combine these ingredients and knead the dough very well — as if you're going to make bread.

Form a dough ball and place it in a deep glass, ceramic, or stainless steal mixing bowl. Cover with cold water and let it rest for an hour or two. This rest period in cold water permits the gluten to firm up.

After the rest, the dough ball should be kneaded gently while still in the bowl under water. This action begins to loosen all the starch, bran, and germ that must be rinsed away to arrive at the remaining gluten. Admittedly, this process does make seitan something of a refined food — but it's still a nutritious meat substitute that comes to you not by way of killing animals or harming the environment.

Back to our bowl. Pour off the white creamy liquid and fill the bowl with fresh water. Resume kneading to continue the process of getting at the gluten. Again, pour off the white liquid that forms. Fill with water and continue this process until only a solid mass of seitan (it sort of looks like a brain) is left in the bowl. The water should then be fairly clear since most of the starch, bran, and germ will have already been washed out.

Remove the seitan and squeeze it firmly to remove any water, then slice it any way you prefer. Simmer these pieces in a broth seasoned with soy sauce, salt, and your favorite herbs and spices. Cooking time will vary depending upon the size and thickness of the seitan pieces. Small pieces may only need to simmer for 15 to 25 minutes, while larger ones may take double or triple that time.

After cooking, allow the seitan pieces to cool in the broth. Then transfer to a covered container, liquid and all, and refrigerate. It'll keep for up to a week — that is, if you somehow can keep your family or friends from wolfing down your entire creation at the next meal.

Slaughterhouse Byproducts

It's been correctly observed that even strict vegetarians aren't able to shun all animal products. That's because slaughterhouse byproducts are nearly everywhere. They're found in the ingredients of such everyday items as cosmetics, soaps, pharmaceuticals, inks, film, rubber products, plastics, paints, textiles, steel products, clothing, brushes, shoes, cardboard, automotive parts, and hundreds more.

In foods, hidden animal byproducts can show up in baked goods (lard — an animal fat); candies, desserts, and some dairy products (gelatin — derived from animal hooves and bones); white sugar (purified with animal bone charcoal); chewing gum (animal fat softeners); cheese (rennin and pepsin — coagulants from animal stomachs); many nonorganic fruits and vegetables (sprayed with animal fat-based waxes); and many others.

It would seem then that slaughterhouse byproducts are essentially unavoidable. But, in abstaining from animal flesh and by dodging as many animal products as possible (reading package labels, buying only cruelty-free products, etc.), vegetarians actually encourage manufacturers that use byproducts to develop nonanimal sources.

In short, the less animal flesh eaten, the fewer animals have to be raised and slaughtered. And this would mean that fewer animal byproducts would be available — resulting in the need to develop alternatives to animal byproducts. Thus, far from being a futile act (as some cynics contend), a vegetarian diet is a powerful tool in the effort to banish the glut of slaughterhouse byproducts that seem to permeate our everyday lives.

Soy Cheese

Would you eat cheese if you knew there was meat in it? Most dairy cheese in America is made either with rennet (sometimes called rennin) or pepsin — which are coagulating enzymes scraped from the stomach linings of slaughtered cows and pigs.

With this in mind, more and more vegetarians are choosing alternatives to dairy products. And soyfoods producers have responded by offering a cornucopia of soy cheeses to choose from.

Chiefly made from soy milk or tofu, soy cheese is considered by many to be a more wholesome product than standard cheese made from cow's milk. Most brands of soy cheese are lower in fat and calories, higher in calcium, contain no cholesterol, are made from superior (often organic) ingredients, and do not require the killing of animals since neither rennet nor pepsin is used (and wouldn't work on soy milk, anyway) as a coagulant.

But, with all that said, there is something about soy cheese that even many vegetarians aren't aware of. Namely, that virtually every soy cheese on the market is composed of about 20 percent casein, a protein derived from cow's milk. Producers add it to soy cheese to make the product stretch and melt when heated — characteristics of dairy cheese.

Unlike rennet, however, the use of casein does not involve slaughtering any cows. Of course, vegans (those who eat no animal products whatsoever) point out that using any animal product, even when no killing is required, is tantamount to supporting the cruel and exploitive practices of the factory farming industry.

On the other hand, it's argued that your eating a product (soy cheese) with only a 20 percent dairy content is far less supportive of the dairy industry than if you ate regular dairy cheese.

Fortunately, one soy food maker offers a soy cheese that's completely free of casein. Called Soymage, this cheese works best if grated and added to cooked dishes. It doesn't melt well and becomes somewhat rubbery if you try to melt it the way you would a cheese containing casein. Other makers are planning similar vegan products that will have more of the taste and texture of dairy cheese.

In closing, it should be pointed out that all soy cheeses (including those brands of "cheese" that use almond milk) are highly processed foods. So, enjoy them — but use them sparingly. Whichever type of cheese you choose, be sure to check the label for ingredients. Many "dairy-free" soy cheeses actually contain casein and possibly artificial additives — things you may want to avoid.

Soy Milk

For those who can't digest milk, or who want to avoid dairy products, soy milk makes a perfect substitute for cow's milk. In nearly every nutritional department, soy milk gets higher marks than milk. For example, soy milk has as much protein and more essential nutrients than milk. What's more, soy milk is lower in fat than milk, much higher in iron, and contains no lactose (the sugar in cow's milk that can cause intestinal problems) or cholesterol. And without any animal fat (which traps toxins) soy milk has far fewer contaminants than cow's milk.

Soy milk can be found in most natural foods stores and supermarkets packaged in aseptic containers that have an incredible shelf life of about one year. Smooth, creamy, and delicious, soy milk is available in several flavors: vanilla, chocolate, carob, or "plain." Use soy milk as you would dairy milk. It's great on cereals, and in cooking, baking, and dessert making. However, some brands definitely taste better than others. Buy a container of each and find the one you like best — and you'll be hooked forever.

If you really want your soy milk fresh — make it yourself at home. There's nothing to it. Rinse several cups of dry, whole soybeans and cover with a few quarts of water in a large container overnight. The next day, drain the plumped beans.

Using a blender, grind one cup of soaked beans with two cups of very warm water. Boiling water is better (it makes the soy milk less "beany" tasting) but you'll need a glass or metal blender container to do so. Grind for a minute or two until each batch is smooth. Then, pour the blended mix through a fine sieve into a large pot. Squeeze out the soy milk in the sieve by pressing the mix with a bottle or jar.

When all the beans have been ground and strained, transfer the soy milk pot to the stove and simmer for about 45 minutes. The soy milk must be cooked in order to inactivate certain bean enzymes that would prevent you from digesting "raw" soy milk. Adding a little oil to the pot helps minimize the foaming during the cooking process.

After the soy milk has been cooked, let it cool before adding any flavorings. Return a quart of this milk to the blender, add the following, and blend:
- 1 tablespoon vegetable oil
- 3 tablespoons maple syrup, honey or organic cane sugar
- 1 teaspoon vanilla
- ⅛ teaspoon salt

Don't be shy to experiment with the flavorings. Add carob or cocoa powder if you wish. Or try more sweeteners if you have a sweet tooth. Blend for about 30 seconds, then transfer the contents to jars and refrigerate immediately. Use your fresh, homemade soy milk in the same way you would the store-bought kind.

Soy Sauce

Most soy sauces made in the U.S. are mass produced in a hurried fashion and contain synthetic ingredients, colorings, preservatives, and flavorings. For these reasons it's best to look elsewhere for vegetarian liquid seasonings.

Far superior to soy sauce are **shoyu** and **tamari** — traditional, naturally brewed "soy sauces" that intensify the flavor of stir-fried vegetables, cooked grains, soups, stews, gravies, tofu or tempeh dishes, and virtually every other savory cuisine.

Since shoyu and tamari basically have the same flavor they may be interchanged in any recipe. However, there are differences between them that go beyond mere taste. Although both are made with naturally fermented soybeans, shoyu is brewed with wheat, while tamari is usually not. It's probably important only for those with wheat allergies to be aware of this (the label on the bottle will confirm whether or not wheat is an ingredient).

Shoyu is not as thick, rich, or full-flavored as tamari and won't hold up as well in cooking. For this reason, shoyu should be added to a dish after cooking; while tamari can be added towards the end of the cooking process. You don't want to add either seasoning at the start of cooking as the heat will radically diminish their exquisite flavors and fragrances.

A word of caution. Both shoyu and tamari, while being excellent alternatives to soy sauce and salt, are high in sodium — so use them sparingly. If sodium intake is a concern, you might try checking your natural foods store for the low-sodium "soy sauces" that are now being produced.

There is another tasty liquid seasoning on the market. Called Bragg Liquid Aminos, this flavoring is recommended for those with yeast allergies since Bragg's is not a fermented product. And just like shoyu and tamari, it can take the place of soy sauces and salt, and will impart a savory, beef-like flavor to whatever dish it's used in.

Although slightly lower in sodium than shoyu and tamari, Bragg's too is a salty seasoning that should be used frugally.

Soy Yogurt

While they aren't exactly like milk-based yogurts, the current crop of soy yogurts will definitely make a favorable impression on the taste buds. Available in plain, vanilla, and fruit-flavors, soy yogurts come packaged in either the 32 ounce or half-pint containers.

These nutritious non-dairy yogurts can be used in all recipes that call for dairy yogurt. These include dishes utilizing sour milk, sour cream, and mayonnaise (the plain yogurt would work best in these). Thick creamy smoothies made up of soy yogurt plus such fresh fruit as strawberries or bananas can easily be whipped up in a blender.

Besides being free of all animal products (no casein, either), soy yogurts contain no white sugar, chemical additives, or cholesterol. Two brands to look for are White

Wave's Dairyless Soy Yogurt and Nancy's Cultured Soy Non-Dairy Yogurt.

Sweeteners

White sugar supplies calories without any nutritional value, causes sudden swings in blood-sugar levels, exacerbates many medical conditions, and rots the teeth. But, it's usually avoided by many vegetarians for another important (but little known) reason.

Namely, because the sugar cane industry actually uses charred cattle bones to filter out impurities from the sugar cane. (The industry claims to have tried other purifiers, but that bone char is the best product for this task.) Whatever the merits of using the bones of slaughtered animals to refine sugar, vegetarians who wish to steer clear of sugar need not deprive their sweet tooth of its just desserts.

Most natural foods stores carry tasty, nutritious sweeteners that are not processed with animal products. These include:

• **Powdered sugar cane juice** is probably the highest quality sweetener you'll find anywhere. It's made by dehydrating sugar cane juice and then milling it into granules. Since only the water is removed, many of the wholesome vitamins, minerals, and elements of the sugar cane are left intact.

The best known brand of powdered sugar cane juice is Sucanat (which stands for sugar cane natural), an unrefined, organic product that looks like brown sugar and has a rich flavor — a bit like molasses. Sucanat can be substituted for white sugar in any recipe.

What's more, studies have shown that Sucanat not only digests much more slowly than white sugar (which keeps your blood-sugar levels from going ballistic), but also doesn't promote dental caries (tooth decay) like white sugar.

• **Brown rice syrup** is a light, delicate-tasting, nutritious sweetener that's made by fermenting brown rice with a natural enzyme and water, and then boiling the liquid until it thickens. Rice syrup, with 50 percent complex carbohydrates, digests very slowly and therefore has a salutary effect on blood-sugar levels.

The syrup looks like honey, but is less sweet. It goes well in sauces, drinks, desserts, and baked goods; and can be used as a spread instead of jelly. Some people think that rice syrup has a flavor similar to butterscotch.

• **Barley malt syrup** is a sweetener made from the boiled liquid of fermented sprouted barley. It looks a lot like molasses but has a much milder taste — almost a caramel flavor, in fact. It's endowed with some of the vitamins and minerals found in whole barley and is rich in complex carbohydrates (making it less likely to cause sugar highs when digested). Barley malt syrup can be used in pastries, sauces, desserts, and anywhere else sweeteners are called for.

• **Date sugar** is made from finely ground, dried dates. It makes a wonderful substitute for granulated white sugar in many recipes. Although it doesn't really dissolve very well, date sugar (with its distinctive date flavor) makes a fine sweetener in baking and cooking.

Incidentally, brown sugar, raw sugar, and turbinado sugar are no health foods. They pretty much undergo the same treatment as white sugar. Brown sugar is nothing more than white sugar with a coloring added. Raw sugar is actually coarse white sugar; and turbinado sugar is white sugar that's a bit less coarse than raw sugar. All in all, basically the same white, unwholesome stuff.

Fructose is another sugar with a healthy image that doesn't quite square with the facts. Although fructose naturally occurs in fruits, it's commercially produced from corn (not from fruits as its name implies). This highly refined sweetener is cheap to manufacture and is used in soft drinks instead of sugar in order to bestow a healthier product image. Perhaps the only kind thing to be said of fructose is that it breaks down in the body much more slowly than white sugar. And this has less of a jolt on the body's metabolism

Tahini

Tahini is one of two thick, creamy pastes made from sesame seeds. The other is **sesame butter**. Tahini is made from raw, hulled sesame seeds; sesame butter is made from toasted, unhulled sesame seeds. While tahini has a light color and mild, delicate taste, sesame butter is a bit darker, thicker, and nuttier (some say "stronger") than tahini. Nutritionally, they're about the same.

These distinctive-tasting sesame pastes (both high in protein and rich in calcium) can be used in many dishes. When combined with puréed garbanzo beans, they create a popular Middle Eastern dip called hummus. Mixed with a little water to dilute their thick textures, sesame pastes can be added to stir-fries, sauces, desserts, steamed vegetables, dressings, baked goods, and a number of other dishes.

If at all possible, try to purchase tahini or sesame butter at a natural foods store. You'll have a better chance of

Appendix I: GLOSSARY

finding a brand that doesn't use chemicals to remove the tiny sesame seed hulls. The label will indicate "chemical-free" if that's the case. While most commercial manufacturers of sesame pastes use lye or other caustic chemicals to dissolve the seed hulls, organic producers use a mechanical process only — which means you don't get any unwholesome residues in your sesame butter and tahini.

Tempeh

Low in calories, as high in protein as beef or chicken, full of fiber, and without a drop of cholesterol, tempeh (pronounced tem-pay) is as fine a meat substitute as you'll come across. This cultured (or fermented) soyfood is made by incubating cooked soybeans with a bacteria that binds the beans and forms a solid mass.

It comes in rectangular cakes and is found either in the refrigerator or freezer section of most natural foods stores. You can substitute tempeh in nearly any recipe that calls for chicken, beef, or fish. Tempeh is firm and chewy with a mild, meaty, mushroomy flavor.

Tempeh should never be eaten raw. If you're going to use it in a stir fry or other quick-cooked dish, the tempeh should be pre-cooked (steamed, simmered or baked) for at least 20 to 25 minutes. If you purchase tempeh frozen, you can either defrost it overnight in the refrigerator, or for a few hours on the kitchen counter right before it's to be cooked. Tempeh is quite perishable, so don't store it in the refrigerator longer than a week before eating. In the freezer, it'll last for several months.

Don't be alarmed by any black or gray spots that may form on the tempeh cakes. These are natural mold growths that won't cause any harm (although some people find it more appetizing to scrape these specks off with a knife). On the other hand, toss out the tempeh if it develops a strong, foul odor or has mold spots of other colors.

Tempeh is ideal for those who usually have intestinal gas problems after eating beans. Since tempeh is a fermented product (its protein and sugars are broken down by the bacteria) most people find it quite easy to digest.

This versatile soyfood can be diced, sliced, cubed, or grated, and added to salads, pastas, soups, casseroles, tacos, spaghetti sauce, stews, chili, or a host of other dishes. Or try slicing it thin, baking it in a sauce (tempeh dries out easily if not baked in a liquid) and then slipping it between whole grain bread slices for a delectable sandwich. Also, many natural foods stores sell pre-cooked tempeh as convenient ready-to-eat "burgers" and "bacon."

To learn lots more about this amazing, nutritious food, I recommend reading *The Book of Tempeh* by William Shurtleff and Akiko Aoyagi (HarperCollins, 1985).

Textured Vegetable Protein (T.V.P.)

T.V.P. is yet another extraordinary product made from processed soybeans. When cooked, it closely resembles meat in appearance and texture — so much so, that most unsuspecting carnivores won't even realize that they're eating a dish of plant foods.

High in protein and certain vitamins and minerals, T.V.P. can easily replace the meat in such dishes as sloppy joes, chili, tacos, burritos, soups, stews, lasagnas — or even as a pizza topping. It's usually sold in natural foods stores as granules and must be reconstituted before using. To do this, just pour one cup of boiling water over the same amount of T.V.P. in a small bowl. Mix thoroughly and let it rest for about ten minutes. Then it's ready to be added to any recipe as a replacement for the meat. Simmered in spicy sauces or vegetarian broths, for example, T.V.P. will eagerly absorb every flavor it encounters.

Although its critics point out that T.V.P. is a highly processed soyfood, it is, after all, completely free of cholesterol, animal fat, and the violence of the slaughterhouse. For these and other reasons, textured vegetable protein can make a fine alternative to meat.

Thickeners and "jell-ers"

Many vegetarians prefer not to cook with gelatin since that product is made from the pulverized hooves, bones, and connective tissue of slaughtered animals. Instead they use such plant-based thickening agents as kudzu, agar-agar, and arrowroot to make fruit desserts, preserves, gravies, sauces, jellies, and puddings. Despite their strange names, these vegetarian products are quite easy to work with.

• **Kudzu** (or kuzu) is the starch from a Japanese vine (the same wild plant that's considered a terrible pest in the American South). It's used to thicken sauces, gravies, soups, jelled desserts, and glazes.

Kudzu, a naturally-processed starch, is a superior alternative to cornstarch which is manufactured using a variety of chemical and bleaching agents. Also, cornstarch leaves a chalky taste and rubbery texture, while kudzu is tasteless and smooth.

Kudzu is usually sold in small chunks which have to be crushed into a powder before measuring. The easiest way to do this is to slip a few kudzu lumps into a small plastic bag and pulverize with a solid object like a bottle or rolling pin.

Generally, use between one and two tablespoons of kudzu per cup — you may have to experiment to come up with the right amounts for the textures you want. Dissolve the kudzu in several tablespoons of cold water before adding it to the simmering liquid you want thickened. Simmer for about five to ten minutes, stirring constantly, until the liquid is thick.

• **Arrowroot**, much like kudzu, is a wholesome substitute for over-processed, chemicalized cornstarch. Made from the root of a tropical plant by the same name, arrowroot is a natural thickener ideal for making soups, sauces, pie fillings, gravies, and puddings.

Since it's tasteless and colorless, arrowroot is perfect for thickening fruit sauces and clear glazes. Typically, one tablespoon of arrowroot powder is used to thicken one cup of liquid. Thicker, firmer textures can be achieved by doubling the amount of powder used for each cup of liquid. Dissolve the arrowroot in a little cold water before adding it to the dish you're preparing. Simmer in a saucepan for five to ten minutes, stirring often until thick.

• **Agar-Agar** (also known as **kanten** or **agar**) is a natural, vegetarian gelatin substitute. Made from sea vegetables, agar is available in bars and flakes — although the flakes are more convenient and yield the more consistent results. Mixed with juice and sliced fruit, agar will make a tasty, wholesome "Jell-O" that's free of gelatin. It can also be used as a thickener in fruit purées, vegetable soups, jams, jellies, sauces, fruit stews, puddings, pie fillings — and in any recipe calling for gelatin.

To use agar, thoroughly dissolve it in cold water before adding it to the simmering liquid to be thickened. Use about one tablespoon of agar flakes for each cup of liquid. Simmer for several minutes and stir occasionally. Pour the mix into a heatproof bowl and allow it to harden at room temperature for about an hour. Or, refrigerate and you'll have a firm, pudding texture in half that time.

Besides being able to mimic gelatin, agar is rich in iron, calcium and other nutrients. It's high in fiber — and studies show that agar bonds with toxic metals in the body and carries them out with each elimination.

Tofu

What could possibly be more versatile than tofu? With its neutral taste and soft consistency, tofu easily picks up the flavors of all the herbs, spices, seasonings, and condiments it encounters. It can be cooked in any number of ways and substituted for meat, cheese, and eggs in most recipes.

Let's back up. What is tofu? It's a highly nutritious and digestible soyfood (often called "bean curd") made from soy milk in much the same way that cheese is made from cow's milk. The process goes something like this. Soy milk is boiled, a coagulant is added to make solids (curds), and then these curds are separated from the whey (liquid) and pressed into tofu blocks.

Generally, tofu is available in either soft or firm varieties. Soft tofu has a higher water content than firm tofu and therefore has a lower nutrient density. Soft tofu, with its custard-like texture, is ideal for dips, sauces, salad dressings, "milk" shakes, puddings, and other desserts. Firm tofu, on the other hand, keeps its shape in cooking and is better suited for stir-fry dishes, scrambled "eggs," casseroles, and sandwich fillers.

Although nearly 50 percent of its calories come from fat, tofu is still an ideal low-calorie food for those watching their weight (only about 20 calories per ounce) — plus it's high in protein and completely lacking in cholesterol.

You'll find tofu usually sold covered with water in sealed packages. Check the "expiration date" to get the freshest tofu possible. At home, remove the tofu from its package, rinse with cold water, and place it in a sealed container that's filled with cold water. Tofu will stay "fresh" under refrigeration for at most a week provided the water is changed daily (or every other day, if you forget).

Fresh tofu is odorless. It you notice a sour smell and taste, or if it's very slippery to the touch, then it's time to toss it out (or take it back to the store if you find these things after opening the package).

Incidentally, you can give tofu a complete make-over by freezing it. Its texture will become spongy and chewy — quite meatlike, in fact. You can freeze tofu overnight in its package or sliced on a plate. A few hours before you need it, allow the frozen tofu to thaw in a colander. (If you're short on time, pour boiling water over the tofu.)

After the tofu has thawed (and cooled if boiling water was used) squeeze out the excess water by pressing the tofu between your hands. It's now ready to be cubed, chunked, or crumbled and added to any number of dishes. Thawed tofu absorbs the flavor of vegetables, herbs, spices, and other seasonings exceptionally well.

A final note. If you're planning to use tofu in a dish that involves no cooking, it's advisable to first boil the tofu for several minutes to kill any bacteria present in the bean curd.

And to learn absolutely everything there is to know about

tofu, just pick up a copy of *The Book of Tofu* by Shurtleff and Aoyagi (see Resources).

Whole Grains

Whole grains are those that still have the **bran** and **germ** layers attached to the **endosperm** layer. This wholesome combination is ideal for human nutritional needs, supplying us with carbohydrates, proteins, minerals, and roughage in just the right proportions.

Steer clear of refined grains and their products (such as white rice and white bread). They've had all the nutritious germ and bran stripped away. Why's that done? Because doing that prolongs the shelf life of the grains and their products. Unfortunately, it also robs the grains of their vital nutrients and all-important fiber.

Walk into any large natural foods store and you'll see bin after bin of various whole grains, including millet, buckwheat, amaranth, barley, bulgur, brown rice, oats, wheat berries, corn, triticale, quinoa, and many others.

Most people choose a few different grains and stick with them. Instead of describing every grain you may encounter, I'd like to cover a few "basic" grains — ones I'm especially fond of — and encourage you to sample them and then branch out to try many of the others as well.

Although cooking instructions vary from grain to grain, you won't go wrong by using 2 cups of liquid for each cup of grains. But before you start cooking, grains need a little preparation. First of all, measure out the grains and spread on a cookie sheet. Then pick out any discolored or badly broken grains (and any other debris that shouldn't be there, like stones) and discard them. Finally, rinse the grains well in a sieve.

Now you're ready to slowly add the grains to the pot of boiling liquid (this method usually keeps the finished product from being mushy). Lower the heat, cover, and simmer until the grains have absorbed all the liquid. Although brown rice takes the longest to cook (about 45 minutes) the other grains that I'll describe can be cooked in about one-third to one-half that time. But, for a more hearty, chewier texture, try cooking these other grains for only 10 minutes; and then turn off the heat and allow the cooked grains to rest for an additional 5 minutes in the covered cooking pot. To get other textures just experiment by varying the amount of liquid used in the cooking process and cooking for longer or shorter times.

Cooked grains can be kept in the refrigerator in a covered container for several days or for longer periods in the freezer. When you first buy your grains, be sure to store them in tightly-sealed containers in a cool place out of direct sunlight. Storing in the refrigerator or freezer is ideal if you can spare the room. Although most grains can last up to a year if properly stored, it's better to purchase smaller quantities and use them up fairly quickly.

• **Brown Rice:** The term "brown rice" can be used to designate any whole grain rice — although, as we'll see, there are many varieties of rice. The three basic types (or lengths) of brown rice are short-grain, medium-grain, and long-grain. While all are equally nourishing, their differences have more to do with taste and texture than with anything else.

• Short-grain kernels are small and plump. When cooked they become soft, tender, slightly sweet, and a bit chewy. Many people find short-grain sticky, making it ideal in casseroles, rice puddings, baked goods, and croquettes.

• Long-grain brown rice, on the other hand, is made of long, slender kernels which cook to a dry, fluffy texture. As the grains remain separate after cooking, long-grain is well-suited for use in bean dishes, salads, and as a bed of grains for stir-fried vegetables. It's the most commonly-eaten brown rice and is found in nearly every type of food store in America.

• Medium-grain, as its name implies, falls somewhere in between the other two. It's often compared with long-grain, although medium grain does cook up more fluffy and tender. It also has more of a sweet, almost-nutty flavor than long-grain. Medium-grain is a good, all-around brown rice that goes well in baked goods and casseroles, in vegetable stuffings, and in many other dishes.

I would be remiss if I failed to describe **brown basmati rice**. This rice has long, slender grains (much like long-grain brown rice) and when cooked will fill up your kitchen (and most of the house) with a delightful fragrance akin to roasting peanuts and popping popcorn. It has a unique nutty flavor and chewy texture; and is appropriate in any recipe calling for either medium-grain or long-grain brown rice.

A walk down the natural foods store aisle may reveal such other rices as sweet rice, wehani rice, wild rice, arborio rice, and white rice. Do try to stay away from white (or polished) rice. With its bran layer and germ removed in processing, white rice is nutritionally inferior to brown rice — and doesn't taste as good, either. Although white rice (like white bread) is often "enriched," only a fraction of the known nutrients are ever put back, however.

With so many brown rices to choose from, why not experiment with each to find which ones will strike your fancy.

• **Buckwheat:** Most natural foods stores carry this grain in two forms: raw buckwheat groats and roasted buckwheat groats. Roasted buckwheat is also known as kasha. (By the way, each individual buckwheat kernel is called a "groat".)

Buckwheat contains high quality protein and is a rich source of many vitamins and minerals, particularly iron and calcium. It's gluten-free making it suitable for those with gluten allergies, and cooks up alkaline which is good news for those with stomach-acid problems.

Yes, but how does it taste? Buckwheat has been described as having a bold flavor and distinctive aroma. This hearty, quick-cooking grain cooks to a soft and fluffy texture. Roasted buckwheat has a stronger, nuttier flavor than the raw groats, which are milder.

Cooked buckwheat groats are quite versatile. They're just right in a stir-fry with onions and mushrooms. As a rice substitute, buckwheat can be added to soups, used to stuff vegetables, and goes well in a number of other "rice" dishes. Or it can simply be eaten as a hot breakfast cereal with your favorite embellishments.

• **Millet:** High in protein, iron, minerals and vitamins, millet is an important life-sustaining staple in China, Africa, and India. It is the food of the famous Hunza people of the Himalayas who are known for their strength, good health, and longevity. In this country, however, millet is usually fed to the birds.

This small, round, golden grain cooks quickly to a light and fluffy consistency. With a mild, nutty flavor, millet can be eaten as a breakfast cereal topped with chopped nuts, dried fruit, and soy milk. Or it can substitute for rice and be added to soups, muffins, casseroles, stuffings, breads, croquettes, and any number of other dishes.

Appendix I: GLOSSARY

As a low-gluten grain, millet is often recommended for those with gluten allergies. Also, since millet becomes alkaline when cooked, it's the grain of preference for many people who suffer from excessive acid production.

If you'd like your breakfast millet crunchy — and I do mean crunchy — use very little water and cook it for a short time. For example, cook one cup of millet in one cup of water in a covered pan for three to five minutes. Let it rest for another five minutes. Then serve topped with fruit, nuts, and soy milk or fruit juice. Chew well.

• **Rolled Oats:** Often referred to as "old-fashioned oatmeal," rolled oats are not only nutritious, they're also an excellent source of soluble fiber known for its healthful effects on blood cholesterol. Rolled oats are made from whole oats (called oat groats) that are first steamed (to soften them up) and then flattened into flakes between steel rollers.

Rolled oats typically are used to make cooked cereal, granola, and oatmeal cookies, as well as to thicken sauces and soups. A popular way of eating rolled oats is as a cold (un-cooked) cereal. Fill a bowl with one cup of rolled eats. Add about a cup of soy milk or almond milk and let the cereal rest for a few minutes until it absorbs all the liquid. Top with dried or fresh fruits, chopped nuts, and a little natural sweetener (such as honey, maple syrup, or sucanat cane sugar). The softened oats have a mild taste and chewy texture. On cold mornings, try this same recipe, but use warm or hot soy milk or almond milk instead.

Avoid the instant (quick-cooking) oatmeals since they have been processed much more than rolled oats and are usually packaged with salt, flavorings, and other additives.

• **Quinoa:** Considered a sacred plant by the ancient Incas of Peru, quinoa (pronounced keen-wa) is a nutritional powerhouse. Along with having the highest protein-content of any grain, quinoa is abundantly endowed with essential amino acids, vitamins, and minerals.

It's very easy to prepare — and to digest. This grain cooks to a fluffy texture and mild, nutty taste. With each chew you'll experience the delicate, crunchy characteristic of cooked quinoa.

Note: Each quinoa grain is covered with a bitter resin coating (called saponin) that protects it from birds and insects. This natural pest-repellent must be thoroughly removed before cooking the grain or you'll wind up with a pungent pot of quinoa. Just before cooking, rinse the quinoa a number of times to flush away the saponin.

Whole Wheat Flour

Wheat is the most widely grown grain on the planet. When eaten as the unrefined product that Mother Nature intended it to be, wheat is packed with nutrition — full of protein, vitamins, minerals and fiber. But when whole wheat is refined and stripped of its valuable bran and germ components (and in some cases, bleached with harsh chemicals to make white flour) it loses over three-fourths of its nutrients and fiber.

Which is why most health-minded vegetarians choose whole wheat flour over white. They also avoid so called "enriched" flours which are nothing more than feeble attempts by flour manufacturers to add back minimal amounts of the known nutrients that were stripped from the whole grains during flour processing.

Whole wheat flour can be found in most natural foods stores in two varieties. One is known as "whole wheat flour," the other as **"whole wheat pastry flour."** Both are nutritious, whole grain flours — each with its own specific use. Whole wheat flour is high in gluten making it ideal for breadmaking. On the other hand, whole wheat pastry flour is lower in gluten and more finely milled, thus making it better suited for pastries, cookies, cakes, and crusts.

Since whole grain flours contain the highly perishable germ and bran layers, they should be stored in airtight containers in a dry, cool place (the freezer or refrigerator would be fine, especially in hot, humid weather). Try to obtain freshly-ground flour if possible. Ask at your natural foods store about that. Fresh flour has a somewhat sweet flavor when you taste a pinch of it. Rancid flour has a bitter taste. Flour that sits in bags on shelves for months will not produce nutritious baked goods. Neither will white flours, since much of their nutrients have been removed — in part to prolong shelf life (without the oily germ, white flour can sit on shelves indefinitely without spoilage).

When substituting whole wheat flour for white, you should know that whole wheat will absorb more liquid than will white flour. Therefore, for each cup of white flour called for in the recipe, just substitute ¾ of a cup of whole wheat flour.

Besides whole wheat flour, your natural foods store may also stock other nourishing whole grain flours, like oat, brown rice, buckwheat, and rye flours. These "alternative" flours make delightful additions to most baked goods. Just replace a small amount of the whole wheat flour with one of these other flours. Recipe books abound with ideas for these lesser known, but tasty flours.

Appendix II

Networking

Vegetarian Organizations

American Vegan Society (AVS)
501 Old Harding Highway
Malaga, NJ 08328
(609) 694-2887

The American Vegan Society is a nonprofit educational organization teaching a compassionate way of living. It advocates a diet and lifestyle that exclude all animal products, such as flesh foods, dairy products, eggs, honey, gelatin, leather, wool, silk, furs, and all others of animal origin.

In order to educate the public on the ethical, ecological, healthful, and economic aspects of veganism, the organization sponsors live-in cooking classes, lectures, discussions, and educational conventions.

Membership is open to all and includes the AVS quarterly publication, plus books, magazines, audio and video tapes, and more at discount prices.

Association of Vegetarian Dietitians and Nutrition Educators (VEGEDINE)
3835 Rt. 414
Burdett, NY 14818

Founded in 1983, VEGEDINE is a nonprofit networking and publishing foundation. It offers a home-study course in Basic Vegetarian/Vegan Nutrition. This correspondence study is geared for both laypersons and health professionals.

Upon successful completion of the 18-unit course, the student will receive a Certificate of Educational Achievement in Vegetarian Nutrition from VEGEDINE.

In addition, VEGEDINE maintains a directory of vegetarian-oriented health professionals and educators. For a copy of this directory send a self-addressed, stamped business envelope to VEGEDINE.

North American Vegetarian Society (NAVS)
P.O. Box 72
Dolgeville, NY 13329
(518) 568-7970

Since its inception in 1974, the North American Vegetarian Society has been dedicated to promoting the joy, compassion, and life-enhancing potential of vegetarianism. It has organized and sponsored annual vegetarian conferences, including several world events — perhaps the most well-known being the annual World Vegetarian Day, held the first day in October.

NAVS members receive the quarterly publication Vegetarian Voice, discounts on books and merchandise, and reduced registration fees at annual conferences.

Vegetarian Nutrition Dietetic Practice Group (VNDPG)
216 W. Jackson Blvd., #800
Chicago, IL 60606
(312) 899-0040 (ext. 4815)

This group provides the latest information on vegetarian nutrition to dietitians, health and food service profession als, and the public. It publishes an excellent quarterly newsletter, sponsors workshops, facilitates educational resource development projects; and provides assistance to those people wishing to locate a vegetarian dietitian in their local area.

Since it's a part of the America Dietetic Association, the VNDPG is open only to fellow registered dietitians who already belong to that Association. However, the general public may subscribe to the group's newsletter "Issues in Vegetarian Dietetics."

Vegetarian Resource Group
P.O. Box 1463
Baltimore, MD 21203
(410) 366-VEGE

The Vegetarian Resource Group is a nonprofit organization whose health professionals, activists, and educators work with businesses and individuals to bring about healthy changes in schools, workplaces, and communities. Its registered dietitians and physicians assist in the development of nutrition related publications and respond to member or media questions about the vegetarian diet.

This organization develops books, brochures, and software for consumers, teachers, and health professionals. It staffs information booths and gives presentations at the annual meetings of many food service, education, and dietetic associations around the country.

In addition, the Vegetarian Resource Group publishes the bimonthly Vegetarian Journal — a magazine containing a cornucopia of practical tips for vegetarian meal planning, articles relevant to vegetarian nutrition, meatless recipes, and natural food product reviews. The Journal discusses the various aspects of a vegetarian diet, including health, environmental, ethical, and economic considerations.

The Group's other publications include Vegetarian Journal's Food Service Update newsletter, and Tips for Vegetarian Activists newsletter. It also sponsors weekend vegetarian gatherings and one-day conferences, and gives generous assistance to those wishing to start local vegetarian groups (as well as much encouragement and support to existing groups.)

Animal Protection and Rights Groups

American Anti-Vivisection Society (AAVS)
801 Old York Rd. #204
Jenkintown, PA 19046
(215) 887-0816

Committed to ending vivisection — medical research which consists of surgery and experiments performed on living animals — the American Anti-Vivisection Society supports non-animal medical research which helps people without abusing animals. Through their educational, completely non-violent campaigns, they promote humane science and demonstrate that animal research is not essential to human health.

Members come from all walks of life — united in their desire to help create a more compassionate and caring world. By joining the AAVS, you'll receive magazines, literature, action alerts, and more. Also they offer a 150-page guide for students who don't wish to participate in classroom dissections or animal experimentation.

Animal Legal Defense Fund (ALDF)
1363 Lincoln Ave.
San Rafael, CA 94901
(415) 459-0885

The Animal Legal Defense Fund, with over 600 attorneys nationwide, is a national nonprofit organization dedicated to expanding the legal rights and protections of animals in research labs, on farms, and in the wild. And by calling its toll-free national Dissection Hotline (800-922-FROG), students who object to animal dissection or experimentation in the classroom can obtain legal advice.

The Fund is supported almost entirely by tax-deductible membership contributions. Members receive the quarterly ALDF newsletter, "The Animals' Advocate," — and the satisfaction of supporting an organization that's present wherever and whenever animals require legal defense against abuse and exploitation.

Farm Animal Reform Movement (FARM)
P.O. Box 30654
Bethesda, MD 20824
(301) 530-1737

The Farm Animal Reform Movement, begun in 1981, is an activist organization which strives to bring farm animal abuse and suffering to an end, as well as to make the public aware of the harmful impact of factory farming on people and the planet.

Some of its activities include demonstrations like the Great American Meatout, Veal Ban Campaign, and World Farm Animal Day. It encourages youthful activists to become involved in the campaign against farm animal cruelty. Members receive the quarterly newsletter The Farm Report.

Farm Sanctuary
P.O. Box 150
Watkins Glen, NY 14891
(607) 583-2225

For nearly a decade, Farm Sanctuary has been extensively investigating, documenting, and exposing farm animal abuses across the country. This national, nonprofit organization has literally saved thousands of abused animals (it operates the only shelters in the country for victims of "food animal" production) and initiated successful campaigns to end exploitation of farm animals.

Farm Sanctuary's animal rescue, education, investigative, and legislative campaigns are made possible by its many dedicated members who donate money as well as their time and skills to helping animals. Also, internships are available to all persons 16 years or older. It's a unique opportunity to work with abused and neglected farm animals at Farm Sanctuary's shelter and education centers. Assignments include caring and feeding farm animals, office work, and conducting educational tours.

Friends of Animals
777 Post Rd.
Darien, CT 06820
(203) 656-1522

Since its inception in 1957, Friends of Animals has been actively working to protect animals from cruelty and abuse. Today, this U.S. based, international nonprofit group is one of the most respected activist organizations in the world.

Their staff, which includes environmental biologists, wildlife and marine mammal experts, legislative specialists, and animal protection activists, translates the needs of animals into fully developed and executed action programs for change.

Major animal protection programs include: implementing breeding controls for cats and dogs; launching anti-fur campaigns; opposing sport hunting, vivisection, pet theft, and the ivory trade; lobbying for marine mammal protection; and safeguarding national wildlife refuges and public lands.

Members receive ActionLine magazine which keeps them informed about current issues and reports what activities Friends of Animals is carrying on.

Fund For Animals
200 West 57th St.
New York, NY 10019
(212) 246-2096

Established in 1967 by renowned author and animal advocate Cleveland Amory, The Fund For Animals is one of America's most active organizations in the fight against animal cruelty. The Fund pursues a varied agenda that includes legal and legislative action, public education, animal rescue, spay/neuter programs, and the maintenance of several animal sanctuaries around the country.

Donor members receive the Fund For Animals Newsletter (three times a year), bulletins, alerts, and other communications on late-breaking animal protection issues. In addition, members receive discounts on animal-related articles available through the Fund's mail order catalogue.

Humane Farming Association (HFA)
1550 California St.
San Francisco, CA 94109
(415) 771-CALF

The Humane Farming Association is a national, nonprofit organization dedicated to protecting consumers from the dangerous misuse of chemicals in food production and eliminating the severe and senseless suffering to which farm animals are subjected.

Association members include public health specialists, veterinarians, consumer advocates, family farmers, and many others — all united for the purpose of ending cruel, factory farming operations. Toward that end, the HFA employs such "tactics" as consumer education, legal action, legislation, and boycotts. Through such efforts, this organization has emerged as a leader in the battle against farm animal abuse.

Humane Society of the United States (HSUS)
2100 L St. NW
Washington, DC 20037
(202) 452-1100

The nation's largest animal advocate organization (with nearly 2 million members strong) undertakes to educate the public to appreciate and show compassion for all animals. Its energized staff lobbies for animal-protection legislation and monitors the enforcement of existing laws.

The Humane Society assists local advocacy groups to improve their operating methods and sheltering duties. In addition, HSUS conducts workshops and seminars for those who work with animals; publishes informative newsletters, magazines, and other reports for members and the public; and carries out a number of significant programs that deal with pet care, the elimination of animal cruelty, the protection of endangered wildlife, and many other issues.

Interfaith Council for the Protection of Animals and Nature
4290 Raintree Lane, NW
Atlanta, GA 30327
(404) 252-9176

Affiliated with the Humane Society of the United States, The Interfaith Council is a national conservation and animal protection group that works to save the natural environment and all the creatures contained within it.

This national organization is composed of individuals of various religious faiths unified by the belief that moral and spiritual obligations require us to work in support of saving "God's Creation." The council strives to influence all organized religions to recognize and address those issues involved in this planet's ecological crisis.

International Society for Animal Rights (ISAR)
421 South State St.
Clarks Summit, PA 18411
(717) 586-2200

Incorporated in 1959, ISAR was the first organization in the world to use the term "animal rights" in a corporate name. This nonprofit, activist group (with over 40,000 members) is committed to achieving for animals the right not to be made victims because they are weak and defenseless.

Among the most determined, hard-working, and tireless of all animal rights organizations, ISAR uses legal, educational, and other professional means in their battle to expose and end animal abuse. They sponsor animal rights conferences, seminars, and symposiums to further heighten public awareness of animal suffering.

Members and contributors receive ISAR newsletters and catalogues brimming with animal rights-oriented merchandise like books, buttons and stickers, pamphlets, accessories, apparel, and videos.

Jews for Animal Rights (JAR)
255 Humphrey St.
Marblehead, MA 01945
(617) 631-7601

Jews for Animal Rights is an educational, activist organization that promotes vegetarianism, the insights of preventive medicine, alternatives to animal research, community action programs, discussion groups, and educational programs. It disseminates information through newsletters, speakers, videos, and publications.

In order to better facilitate its educational goals, JAR established Micah Publications as its publishing arm. Micah offers a wide array of books on animal rights, and vegetarianism. It also offers a unique series of booklets for Jewish students, rabbis, educators, and parents that explore what Judaism teaches with respect to animal rights, vegetarianism, environmentalism, and other social and global issues.

National Alliance For Animals (NAA)
P.O. Box 77591
Washington, DC 20013
(703) 837-1203

Through public education and political advocacy, the National Alliance For Animals undertakes to defend the inherent value of all life. As a professional, moderate, consensus-building organization, the NAA champions animal rights by working closely with activists, governmental bodies, legislatures, corporations, and other public and private groups.

Among its numerous credits, the Alliance organized the March for the Animals — the largest international event in the history of the animal protection movement — with over 50,000 people gathering in Washington, D.C.

National Anti-Vivisection Society (NAVS)
53 W. Jackson Blvd. #1552
Chicago, IL 60604
(800) 888-NAVS

Since 1929, this charitable, educational, nonprofit organization has been educating the public about the cruelty and waste of animal life in product testing, biomedical research, and classroom demonstrations. Over the years, the National Anti-Vivisection Society has become the largest anti-vivisection group in the country.

Towards its objective of working for the abolition of vivisection and animal abuse, NAVS encourages researchers, physicians, manufacturers, and teachers to discontinue animal testing in favor of tissue cultures, computer and mathematical models, and other alternatives.

Members receive the NAVS Bulletin, local group support, and educational videos on a free loan basis.

People for The Ethical Treatment Of Animals (PETA)
P.O. Box 42516
Washington, DC 20015
(301) 770-PETA

This nonprofit charitable organization, based in the nation's capital, is the fastest growing animal rights group in the United States. Its dedicated members, almost one-half million in all, have done as much to protect animals from exploitation and cruelty as any other group on earth.

PETA provides information on a wide range of topics, such as factory farming, vegetarianism, hunting and trapping, animal experimentation, and cruelty-free cosmetics and household products. They lend or sell video tapes and offer a mail order catalogue that's stocked with an impressive array of animal rights merchandise.

For a nominal charge, you can join PETA and receive their quarterly news magazine, action alerts and updates, merchandise discounts, and more.

PETA Kids
P.O. Box 42516
Washington, DC 20015
(301) 770-PETA

A young offshoot of People For The Ethical Treatment Of Animals, PETA Kids affords youngsters of all ages the opportunity to become a part of the animal rights movement. By joining PETA Kids (it's $3 — or "whatever you can afford") young people will receive a membership card, semi-annual issues of PETA Kids magazine, regular issues of "We're all Animals," and plenty of information on how to help animals.

United Poultry Concerns (UPC)
P.O. Box 59367
Potomac, MD 20859
(301) 948-2406

United Poultry Concerns, a nonprofit public information organization, promotes the compassionate and respectful treatment of domestic fowl. Founded in 1990 by Dr. Karen Davis, this unique organization endeavors to make the public aware of the ways poultry are being used and how these uses profoundly affect human health, ethics, education, and the environment.

UPC disseminates their message through public talks, writings, mailings, conferences, public displays, and film presentations. Members receive the informative quarterly newsletter (Poultry Press) and other timely announcements. Also, books, postcards, videos, and t-shirts are available by mail order.

Nutrition Education Organizations

American Holistic Medical Association (AHMA)
4101 Lake Boone Trail, #201
Raleigh, NC 27607
(919) 787-5146

Holistic Medicine is a philosophy of medical care which emphasizes personal responsibility and fosters a cooperative relationship among all those involved. It encompasses all safe modalities of diagnosis and treatment while emphasizing the whole person — physical, mental, emotional and spiritual.

The American Holistic Medical Association was founded in 1978 to unite licensed physicians who practice holistic medicine. Membership is open to medical doctors, doctors of osteopathy, medical students studying for those degrees, and state licensed, state certified, state registered health care practitioners. (By contacting the Association, members of the public may request a referral listing of AHMA member physicians and health care providers in each state.)

The mission of AHMA is to support practitioners in their evolving personal and professional development and to promote an art and science which acknowledges all aspects of the individual, the family and the planet.

The American Holistic Medical Foundation was founded in 1980 to promote education and research in the field of holistic medicine. The Foundation is open to all individuals and organizations.

American Holistic Veterinary Medical Association (AHVMA)
2214 Old Emmorton Rd.
Bel Air, MD 21015
(410) 569-0795

Holistic Veterinary Medicine uses a wide range of alternative, humane techniques to find the true cause of disease and effect the cure. The whole picture of the patient is taken into consideration — including the environment, the disease pattern, the relationship between the animal and human companions, genetics, nutrition, hygiene, and stress.

The American Holistic Veterinary Medical Association is an organization which functions as a forum for the exploration of alternative areas of health care in veterinary medicine. Anyone wishing to take an animal to a holistic veterinary practitioner can get the names of local holistic vets by sending a self-addressed, stamped envelope to AHVMA.

Center for Science in the Public Interest (CSPI)
1875 Connecticut Ave. NW, #300
Washington, DC 20009
(202) 332-9110

Founded in 1971, the Center for Science in the Public Interest is an advocacy group intent upon improving food safety and nutrition in America. It monitors those regulatory agencies responsible for insuring a safe food supply. When necessary, the Center has filed lawsuits to keep dangerous and poorly tested food items from reaching the marketplace.

Other areas in which it has become involved include improved food labeling practices, and banning deceptive advertising aimed at young people.

Physicians Committee for Responsible Medicine (PCRM)
P.O. Box 6322
Washington, DC 20015
(202) 686-2210

The Physicians Committee for Responsible Medicine, established in 1985, is a nonprofit educational organization supported by a membership of over 3,000 physicians and 60,000 laypersons. PCRM promotes good nutrition, preventive medicine, ethics in human research, better medical care for disenfranchised groups, and alternatives to animal experimentation.

Members receive Good Medicine, the organization's quarterly magazine, and are entitled to discounts on a wide variety of nutrition booklets, audio tapes, posters, books, fact sheets, and magazines.

The Soyfoods Center
P.O. Box 234
Lafayette, CA 94549
(510) 283-2991

Authors William Shurtleff and Akiko Aoyagi Shurtleff (*The Book of Tofu, The Book of Miso, The Book of Tempeh,* and others) began the Soyfoods Center in 1976 as a way of introducing soyfoods to the Western world. Today, the Center is the world's leading source of information on soybeans and soyfoods. It has a library of 35,000 documents and produces three computerized databases — the largest of which, called SoyaScan Publications, is a bibliographic database with more than 40,000 documents covering 3,000 years of soybean and soyfoods production.

Vegetarian Education Network (VE-NET)
P.O. Box 3347
West Chester, PA 19380
(717) 529-8638

The Vegetarian Education Network is an all-volunteer, nonprofit organization dedicated to promoting the vegetarian perspective in schools through education and school lunches. Also, VE-NET sponsors local events and serves as an information source for schools and the general public.

In addition, the Vegetarian Education Network publishes HOW ON EARTH! (HOE!), a unique quarterly publication written by and for youth who support compassionate, ecologically sound living. HOE! features vegetarian recipes, lifestyle and nutrition information, poetry, artwork, and advice covering a wide range of areas of interest to teenagers.

Environmental Organizations

Earth Island Institute
300 Broadway, #28
San Francisco, CA 94133
(415) 788-3666

Founded in 1982, this nonprofit organization develops innovative projects for the conservation, preservation, and restoration of the global environment. Its network of innovative activists focuses on specific environmental threats and offers creative, effective solutions. In little more than a decade, Earth Island has produced remarkable results in many areas, including environmental restoration, endangered species, and energy sustainability.

Members receive the award-winning Earth Island Journal as well as periodic updates on Earth Island campaigns.

EarthSave
706 Frederick St.
Santa Cruz, CA 95062
(408) 423-4069

Author John Robbins founded EarthSave not only to educate the public about the powerful effects that food choices have on health, the environment, and all living things on earth, but also to support people in moving toward a plant-based diet.

This nonprofit health and environmental educational organization encourages sound nutrition, conservation of resources, and sustainable agriculture. It does so through books, audio and video tapes, speaking tours, local action groups, school nutrition and environmental programs, conferences, seminars, workshops, and wilderness outings.

Members receive EarthSave's quarterly publication, discounts on books, tapes, and other items, special offers, and participation in local EarthSave group activities and special events.

Institute For Food and Development
145 9th St.
San Francisco, CA 94103
(800) 888-3314

Also known as Food First, this education activist organization focuses on the social and economic causes of world hunger. It seeks to empower people with the necessary means to assume control of their food resources and effectively end world hunger.

Co-founded by Frances Moore Lappé (author of *Diet for a Small Planet*), the Institute publishes a number of books, pamphlets, and other educational materials in support of its objective to end world hunger. Members receive newsletters, a calendar of events, and research updates.

Rainforest Action Network (RAN)
450 Sansome, #700
San Francisco, CA 94111
(415) 398-4404

The Rainforest Action Network is a nonprofit activist organization dedicated to saving the world's rainforests and protecting the rights of indigenous peoples. Founded in 1985, the Rainforest Action Network works with environmental and human rights groups in 60 countries on major campaigns to protect rainforests and their inhabitants.

RAN members receive Action Alerts — monthly updates on key rainforest issues — as well as the Network's quarterly publication called World Rainforest Report. Their mail-order catalogue is filled with hundreds of unique, rainforest-inspired products — some of which were produced by indigenous peoples who live in the rainforest.

Youth For Environmental Sanity
706 Frederick St.
Santa Cruz, CA 95062
(408) 459-9344

The nonprofit Youth for Environmental Sanity (also known simply as YES!) is a multi-ethnic team of young vegetarian activists who tour the country sharing the information and skills necessary for students to work in positive ways for a healthier planet.

YES! travels to hundreds of public schools each year performing mock game-show skits and presenting slide shows that electrify youthful audiences. Their stimulating presentations educate, inspire, and empower young people to help make the world a better place.

YES! newsletters are sent to every school that's ever hosted a YES! presentation, as well as to YES! donors, members, and local organizers. The newsletters include updates on YES! projects, urgent global issues, and tangible action ideas.

Also, YES! summer training camps, located throughout the country, afford young people the opportunity to obtain in-depth environmental education and training in leader-ship, and skills in community organizing and public speaking.

As a result of countless YES! tours, many students in

America and around the world have become inspired to start YES! presentations in their own communities. With the help and support from YES!, who act as advisors and trainers to local groups, young people everywhere are becoming involved and motivating each other to solve the problems affecting our society and planet.

Magazines

The Animals' Agenda
P.O. Box 25881
Baltimore, MD 21224
(410) 675-4566

The Animals' Agenda is a leading magazine of the animal rights movement. This bimonthly publication is committed to informing the public about animal rights and cruelty-free living for the purpose of inspiring action for animals. Each issue contains informative articles, international news, practical advice, interviews, and more.

Delicious!
1301 Spruce St.
Boulder, CO 80302
(303) 939-8440

This monthly magazine of natural living contains a storehouse of helpful information for those wishing to take responsibility for their health and well-being. The Delicious! staff provides the latest medical and scientific research in a practical, clear, easy-to-understand format. Each issue contains features which cover up-to-the-minute health news, natural healing methods, personal care,

herbal remedies, sports, and healthful cuisine from around
the world.

Natural Health
P.O. Box 1200
Brookline Village, MA 02147
(617) 232-1000

Natural Health is a bimonthly magazine that provides
practical information, new discoveries, and current trends
about natural health and living. Topics include natural
foods and medicine, alternative health care, nutrition,
wellness, personal fitness, and modern holistic teachings.

Veggie Life
Box 57159
Boulder, CO 80322

Veggie Life is a bright, new bimonthly magazine featuring
healthy, vegetarian fare that fits in with today's active
lifestyles. Each issue is packed full of information not only
on cooking, but also on growing a cornucopia of foods
guaranteed to tantalize anyone's taste buds.

Readers may be invited to try out simple, but tasty,
recipes; whip up creamy puddings without any fat; learn
more about MSG, meatless cooking, or even growing
cherimoyas (exotic, heart-shaped subtropical fruit).

Vegetarian Gourmet
P.O. Box 7641
Riverton, NJ 08077

This quarterly magazine delivers completely on its objective of making each issue a model of "easy and healthy"

cooking. It's packed with glossy, vibrant graphics and timely articles. Recipes go beyond a discussion of ingredients, preparation, and taste — they hone in on nutrition, as well.

Regular departments feature healthy fast foods, good sense nutrition, readers' recipes (especially low-fat and no-fat), book reviews, ingredient substitutes, a gourmet glossary, and lots of innovative cooking ideas. And Vegetarian Gourmet's Cook For Kids section is ideal for such things as all-vegetarian birthday parties and other outings.

Vegetarian Times
P.O. Box 570
Oak Park, IL 60303
(708) 848-8100

Vegetarian Times is a monthly magazine that features valuable advice and news items for contemporary vegetarians — newcomers and old-timers, alike — and for those desiring to adopt a meatless lifestyle.

Each issue is packed with practical information on buying and preparing whole foods, plus articles on diet, nutrition, travel, and vegetarian celebrities. Vegetarian Times is considered by many to be America's leading natural foods magazine.

Mail Order Suppliers

Natural Foods

Arrowhead Mills
P.O. Box 2059
Hereford, TX 79045

Deer Valley Farms
RD1
Guilford, NY 13780

Frankferd Farms
318 Love Rd., RD 1
Valencia, PA 16059

Garden Spot Distributors
Rt. 1, Box 729 A
New Holland, PA 17557

Harvest Direct
P.O. Box 4514
Decatur, IL 62525

Jaffe Brothers, Inc.
P.O. Box 636
Valley Center, CA 92082

Mountain Ark Trader
120 South East Ave.
Fayetteville, AR 72701

Organic Farms
10726-B Tucker St.
Beltsville, MD 20705

Walnut Acres
Penns Creek, PA 17862

Vegetarian Pet Foods

Evolution Pet Health Food
2950 Metro Dr., #102
Bloomington, MN 55425
(612) 858-8329

Famous Fido's Specialty Foods
1533 W. Devon Ave.
Chicago, IL 60660
(312) 761-6029

Harbingers of a New Age
717 E. Missoula Ave.
Troy, MT 59935
(800) 884-6262

Pet Guard
P.O. Box 728
Orange Park, FL 32067
(800) 874-3221 [in Florida (800) 331-7527]

Sojourner Farms
P.O. Box 8062
Ann Arbor, MI 48107
(800) 76-SOJOS

Wow-Bow Distributors
13B Lucon Dr.
Deer Park, NY 11729
(516) 254-6064 [outside New York (800) 326-0230]

Clothing, Shoes, and Accessories (No Animal Contents)

Aesop, Inc.
Box 315
Cambridge, MA 02140
(717) 628-8030

Amberwood
Route 2, Box 300
Milford Rd., Baker County
Leary, GA 31762
(912) 792-6246

Beauty Without Cruelty
175 W. 12th St.
New York, NY 10011
(212) 989-8073

Creatureless Comforts
Page Street Enterprises
702 Page St.
Stoughton, MA 02072
(617) 344-7496

Heartland Products, Ltd.
P.O. Box 218
Dakota City, IA 50529

The Warm Store
12 Tannery Brook Rd.
Woodstock, NY 12498
(800) 889-WARM

Appendix III
Resources

Bibliography

Akers, Keith. *A Vegetarian Sourcebook*. Vegetarian Press, 1989.

Amato, Paul (Ph.D.) and Partridge, Sonia. *The New Vegetarians*. Plenum Press, 1989.

Ballentine, Rudolph (M.D.). *Transition To Vegetarianism*. Himalayan Publications, 1987.

Barnard, Neal (M.D.). *Food For Life (How The New Four Food Groups Can Save Your Life)*. Random House, 1993.

Barnard, Neal (M.D.). *The Power of Your Plate*. Book Publishing Co., 1990.

Bruder, Roy (Ph.D.). *Discovering Natural Foods*. Woodbridge Press, 1982.

Coats, C. David. *Old MacDonald's Factory Farm*. The Continuum Publishing Co., 1989.

Diamond, Harvey and Marilyn. *Fit For Life*. Warner Books, Inc., 1985.

East West Journal, 1987-1991.

East West Natural Health, 1992-1993.

Elliot, Rose. *The Vegetarian Mother and Baby Book.* Pantheon Books, 1986.

Gross, Joy. *Raising Your Family Naturally.* Lyle Stuart, Inc., 1983.

Hartbarger, Neil and Janie. *Eating For The Eighties.* Saunders Press, 1981.

Klaper, Michael (M.D.). *Pregnancy, Children, and the Vegan Diet.* Gentle World, Inc., 1987.

Klaper, Michael (M.D.). *Vegan Nutrition: Pure and Simple.* Gentle World, Inc., 1992.

Lappé, Frances Moore. *Diet for a Small Planet.* Ballantine Books, 1991.

Mason, Jim and Singer, Peter. *Animal Factories.* Crown Publishers, 1990.

McDougall, John (M.D.). *McDougall's Medicine: A Challenging Second Opinion.* New Century Publishers, 1985.

Moore, Shirley (Ph.D.) and Byers, Mary. *A Vegetarian Diet.* Woodbridge Press, 1978.

Natural Health magazine, 1993-1994.

Null, Gary. *The Vegetarian Handbook.* St. Martin's Press, 1987.

Ornish, Dean (M.D.). *Dr. Dean Ornish's Program For Reversing Heart Disease.* Random House, 1990.

Peden, Barbara Lynn. *Dogs & Cats Go Vegetarian.* Harbinger House, 1988.

Peden, James. *Vegetarian Cats and Dogs*. Harbingers of a New Age, 1992.

Pennington, Jean (Ph.D., R.D.) and Church, Helen. *Food Values of Portions Commonly Used*, 14th Edition. Harper & Row, 1985.

Pitcairn, Richard (Ph.D.). *Dr. Pitcairn's Complete Guide To Natural Health For Dogs and Cats*. Rodale Press, 1982.

Regan, Tom. *The Case For Animal Rights*. University of California Press, 1983.

Reuben, David (M.D.). *Everything You Always Wanted To Know About Nutrition*. Simon and Schuster, 1978.

Robbins, John. *Diet For A New America*. Stillpoint Publishing, 1987.

Robbins, John. *May All Be Fed: Diet For A New World*. Avon, 1993.

Robertson, Laurel and Flinders, Carol and Ruppenthal, Brian. *The New Laurel's Kitchen*. Ten Speed Press, 1986.

Rose, Joel. *The Vegetarian Connection*. Facts On File Publications, 1985.

Scharfenberg, John (M.D.). *Problems With Meat*. Woodbridge Press, 1989.

Schwartz, Richard (Ph.D.). *Judaism and Vegetarianism*. Micah Publications, 1988.

Shandler, Michael and Nina. *The Complete Guide and Cookbook For Raising Your Child As A Vegetarian.* Ballantine Books, 1986.

Singer, Peter. *Animal Liberation.* The New York Review, 1975.

Singer, Peter. *In Defense of Animals.* Basil Blackwell, Inc., 1985.

Sussman, Vic. *The Vegetarian Alternative.* Rodale Press, 1978.

Thrash, Agatha (M.D.) and Calvin (M.D.). *Nutrition For Vegetarians.* Thrash Publications, 1982.

Vegetarian Journal (Vegetarian Resource Group), 1988-1994.

Vegetarian Times magazine, 1987-1994.

Wasserman, Debra and Mangels, Reed (Ph.D.). *Simply Vegan.* Vegetarian Resource Group, 1991.

Yntema, Sharon. *Vegetarian Baby.* McBooks Press, 1980.

Yntema, Sharon. *Vegetarian Children.* McBooks Press, 1987.

Recommended Books on Vegetarianism and Related Subjects

Akers, Keith. *A Vegetarian Sourcebook*. Vegetarian Press, 1989.

Amory, Cleveland. *Man Kind?* Harper & Row, 1974.

Barnard, Neal (M.D.). *Food For Life (How The New Four Food Groups Can Save Your Life)*. Random House, 1993.

Barnard, Neal (M.D.). *The Power of Your Plate*. Book Publishing Co., 1990.

Coats, C. David. *Old MacDonald's Factory Farm*. The Continuum Publishing Co., 1989.

Diamond, Harvey and Marilyn. *Fit For Life*. Warner Books, Inc., 1985.

Fox, Michael W. (Ph.D., D.Sc.). *Agricide: The Hidden Crisis That Affects Us All*. Schocken Books, 1986.

Fox, Michael W. (Ph.D., D.Sc.). *Inhumane Society: The American Way of Exploiting Animals*. St. Martin's Press, 1990.

Klaper, Michael (M.D.). *Pregnancy, Children, and the Vegan Diet*. Gentle World, Inc., 1987.

Klaper, Michael (M.D.). *Vegan Nutrition: Pure and Simple*. Gentle World, Inc., 1992.

Lappé, Frances Moore. *Diet for a Small Planet*. Ballantine Books, 1991.

Mason, Jim and Singer, Peter. *Animal Factories*. Crown Publishers, 1990.

McDougall, John (M.D.). *McDougall's Medicine: A Challenging Second Opinion*. New Century Publishers, 1985.

McDougall, John (M.D.). *The McDougall Program: 12 Days To Dynamic Health*. NAL-Dutton, 1990.

Newkirk, Ingrid. *Save The Animals: 101 Easy Things You Can Do*. Warner Books, 1990.

Null, Gary. *The Vegetarian Handbook*. St. Martin's Press, 1987.

Ornish, Dean (M.D.). *Dr. Dean Ornish's Program For Reversing Heart Disease*. Random House, 1990.

Rifkin, Jeremy. *Beyond Beef*. Dutton, 1992.

Robbins, John. *Diet For A New America*. Stillpoint Publishing, 1987.

Robbins, John. *May All Be Fed: Diet For A New World*. Avon, 1993.

Shandler, Michael and Nina. *The Complete Guide and Cookbook For Raising Your Child As A Vegetarian*. Ballantine Books, 1986.

Singer, Peter. *In Defense of Animals*. Basil Blackwell, Inc., 1985.

Sussman, Vic. *The Vegetarian Alternative*. Rodale Press, 1978.

Vegetarian Resource Group. *Vegetarian Journal's Guide To Natural Foods Restaurants in the U.S. and Canada.* Avery Publishers, 1993.

Wasserman, Debra and Mangels, Reed (Ph.D.). *Simply Vegan.* Vegetarian Resource Group, 1991.

Yntema, Sharon. *Vegetarian Baby.* McBooks Press, 1980.

Yntema, Sharon. *Vegetarian Children.* McBooks Press, 1987.

Recommended Vegetarian Cookbooks

Davis, Karen (Ph.D.). *Instead of Chicken, Instead of Turkey: A Poultryless "Poultry" Potpourri.* Book Publishing Co., 1993.

Diamond, Marilyn. *The American Vegetarian Cookbook.* Warner Books, 1990.

Dinshah, Freya. *The Vegan Kitchen.* American Vegan Society, 1987.

Goldbeck, Nikki and David. *Nikki and David Goldbeck's American Wholefoods Cuisine.* New American Library, Inc., 1983.

Katzen, Mollie. *Moosewood Cookbook.* Ten Speed Press, 1992.

Madison, Deborah. *The Savory Way.* Bantam, 1990.

McDougall, John (M.D.) and Mary. *The New McDougall Cookbook.* NAL-Dutton, 1993.

PETA and Newkirk, Ingrid. *The Compassionate Cook.* Warner Books, 1993.

Pickarski, Brother Ron. *Friendly Foods.* Ten Speed Press, 1991.

Robertson, Laurel and Flinders, Carol and Ruppenthal, Brian. *The New Laurel's Kitchen.* Ten Speed Press, 1986.

Sass, Lorna. *Recipes From An Ecological Kitchen: Healthy Meals For You and The Planet.* William Morrow and Co., Inc., 1992.

Shurtleff, William and Aoyagi, Akiko. *The Book of Tofu.* Ballantine Books, 1990.

Vegetarian Times. *Vegetarian Times Cookbook.* Macmillan, 1984.

Wasserman, Debra and Mangels, Reed (Ph.D.). *Simply Vegan.* Vegetarian Resource Group, 1991.

About the Author

David A. Gabbe, author of several books, is a former investigator with the Internal Revenue Service and U.S. Department of Labor. A practicing vegetarian for nearly 20 years, he has taught vegetarian cooking, written newspaper features on meatless diets, and co-founded the Portland (Oregon) Vegetarian Group.

Together with his wife, Carolyn, and two children (all seasoned vegetarians), David resides in Oregon's verdant Willamette Valley.

Index

drowsiness, 92-93
hydrogenated, 80
measuring deceptions, 188-193
meat, 5, 78
misleading studies and
claims, 186-187, 189-195
monounsaturated, 80
needs, 81
percentage of calories,
188-189
polyunsaturated, 80
rheumatoid arthritis, 104
saturated, 80
slim vegetarians, 94-96
standard American diet, 81
vegetarian sources, 82
fiber
cancer, 91
flatulence, 19
iron absorption, 60
flatulence, 19
Food First, 252
free radicals, 10-12
Friends of Animals, 241
frozen desserts (dairy free),
206-207
Fund For Animals, 242

Hitler, Adolph, 30
hospitals
vegetarian food, 171-172
human anatomy
carnivore's anatomy, 106-108
natural plant eaters, 106-108
Humane Farming Association,
242
Humane Society of the U.S.,
243

impotence, 88
inhumane slaughter of animals,
124-125
Institute For Food and Development, 253
Interfaith Council for the Protection of Animals and
Nature, 243-244
International Society for
Animal Rights, 244
iron, 52-61
absorption problems, 59-60
amount needed, 55
boosting intake, 61
plant foods, 54
vegetarian intake, 52-53
vitamin C connection, 54
sources, 56-58

Jews for Animal Rights, 245

Klaper, Dr. Michael, 187
kudzu, 223

Lappé, Frances Moore, 36, 253
life expectancy myth, 184

magazines, 255-257
mail order suppliers
clothing, shoes, and accessories (no animal
contents), 260
natural foods, 258
vegetarian pet foods, 259
McDougall, Dr. John, 89, 146,
187

Vegetarian Journal, 238
vegetarian pet foods suppliers, 259
Vegetarian Organizations
American Vegan Society, 235
North American Vegetarian Society, 236
VEGEDINE, 236
Vegetarian Education Network, 251
Vegetarian Nutrition Dietetic Practice Group, 237
Vegetarian Resource Group, 237-238
Vegetarian Nutrition Dietetic Practice Group, 237
Vegetarian Resource Group, 237-238
vegetarians
animal dissection, 166-167
animal products, 129
at work, 161
athletes, 29
bone density, 66-68
calcium intake, 62-63
carnivorous guests, 160
defined, 12-13, 25-26
dinner invitations, 157-159
earliest ancestors, 105
famous persons, 28-29
Hitler myth, 30
hospital food, 171-172
immune system, 4
iron intake, 52
lack of cancer, 91
lack of obesity, 94-95
longevity, 1, 8-10
"mixed" marriages, 162-164
musicians, 29
ovo-lacto, 14
peer-pressure, 164-165

protein consumption, 31
reasons for becoming, 15-18
strict, 14
travelling, 168-170
T.V. and film stars, 28
World War II Danes, 77
writers, 29
Vegetarian Times, 257
Veggie Life, 256
vitamin B12
amount needed, 48-49
deficiency, 49
nursing mothers, 52
pregnancy, 137-138
sources, 47-48, 50
vegans 46, 49

whole grains
basics, 227-228
brown basmati rice, 229
brown rice, 228
buckwheat, 230
millet, 230
quinoa, 232
rolled oats, 231
whole wheat flour, 232-233
whole wheat pastry flour, 233
World Vegetarian Day, 236

Youth For Environmental Sanity, 254-255